D1233537

WHO NEEDS
CLASSICAL MUSIC?

WHO NEEDS CLASSICAL MUSIC?

Cultural Choice and Musical Value

Julian Johnson

OXFORD

UNIVERSITY PRESS

2002

OXFORD

UNIVERSITY PRESS

Oxford   New York
Auckland   Bangkok   Buenos Aires   Cape Town   Chennai
Dar es Salaam   Delhi   Hong Kong   Istanbul   Karachi   Kolkata
Kuala Lumpur   Madrid   Melbourne   Mexico City   Mumbai   Nairobi
São Paulo   Shanghai   Singapore   Taipei   Tokyo   Toronto

and an associated company in Berlin

Copyright © 2002 by Oxford University Press, Inc.

Published by Oxford University Press, Inc.
198 Madison Avenue, New York, New York 10016

www.oup.com

Oxford is a registered trademark of Oxford University Press

Library of Congress Cataloging-in-Publication Data
Johnson, Julian.
Who needs classical music? : cultural choice and musical value / Julian Johnson.
p.   cm.
Includes bibliographical references and index.
ISBN 0-19-514681-6
1. Music—Philosophy and aesthetics.
2. Music—Social aspects.
I. Title.
ML3800 .J64 2002
781.6'8'013—dc21   2001036632

3 5 7 9 8 6 4

Printed in the United States of America
on acid-free paper

FOR BEN AND SAM

ACKNOWLEDGMENTS

THIS BOOK IS the result of over twenty years spent playing music, writing music, listening to music, thinking about music, talking about music, and reading and writing about music. In that time, my musical experiences and my thoughts about music have been shaped by more significant encounters than I could begin to list. For two decades of rich music-making and vivid intellectual inquiry, I owe many debts of gratitude to my teachers, colleagues, students, family, and friends.

In an effort to keep my text as clear as possible, I have omitted the usual academic practice of referencing other writers by means of footnotes. A bibliography lists works that were helpful to me, directly or indirectly, in writing my own. It is offered as an idiosyncratic set of suggestions for further reading. While my own text avoids direct engagement even with these authors, readers with a knowledge of musical aesthetics will recognize the almost constant presence of Theodor W. Adorno. Although I have deliberately avoided dealing with his writings explicitly, the broad thrust of his ideas is evident throughout, and I acknowledge here my profound intellectual debt to his work.

But my single most important influence here, and the person to whom my final acknowledgment is made, is Simon Johnson—conductor, chorus master, teacher, and my father. At his death in 1993, he left unfinished a manuscript for a book on music he intended to call "The Capacity of Wonder." I have never seen the manuscript, but the title aptly sums up his life as a musician and as a teacher and goes to the heart of what he bequeathed to those who came into contact with him: a vision of music that develops our capacity to exceed the boundaries of our mundane lives and revivifies our sense of being part of a greater reality. His approach to music informs the core of this book.

CONTENTS

WHO NEEDS
CLASSICAL MUSIC?

INTRODUCTION

THIS BOOK IS about the value of classical music. More particularly, it is about its apparent devaluation today and the consequences of its current legitimation crisis. But this is merely the starting point for examining classical music's claim to a distinctive value and assessing the relevance that claim retains for our postmodern, plural, and multicultural world. It addresses questions not just about music but about the nature of contemporary culture, because changing perceptions of classical music have less to do with the music itself than with changes in other cultural practices, values, and attitudes. To ask questions about the status of classical music today is inevitably to ask questions about cultural choices more generally. What is the significance of our musical choices? What cultural values do those choices exhibit? Do the cultural values we hold as musical consumers equate with the values with which we align ourselves in other areas, such as education or politics? What is it about classical music that makes it so marginal and about popular music that makes it so central to contemporary society?

But my concern is with classical music, not with popular culture. I have largely avoided the labyrinthine arguments about their competing claims to value because my main point is that while some classical music can and does function as popular culture, its distinctive value lies elsewhere. It makes a claim to a distinctive value because it lends itself to functions that, on the whole, popular music does not, just as popular music lends itself to functions that, on the whole, classical music does not. This different potential of musical types arises not just from how people approach different kinds of music but from the objective differences between musical pieces and musical styles themselves. Central to my argument is the idea that classical music is distinguished by a self-conscious attention to its own musical language. Its claim to function *as art* derives from its peculiar concern with its own materials and their formal patterning, aside from any considerations about its audience or its social use.

In this, my approach differs from studies based in sociology or cultural studies. From these perspectives, music is almost always discussed in terms of its social use and the meanings that are attributed to it in specific social contexts. While this is certainly an important area, it tends to exclude considerations of the music itself. While not ignoring the question of social use, my concern is rather to bring such outward facts of everyday life into tension with a discussion of the music itself. My argument is that musical objects themselves suggest a degree of elaboration and richness of meaning that not only exceeds our habitual use of them but also implies an opposition to the uses to which they are often put.

My use of the term "value" is therefore not neutral. I am not primarily interested in the way value is conferred on music through the local, evaluative practices that are the proper concern of sociology. My question is not why different people find different music valuable, but rather how different musics themselves articulate different values and the extent to which these correlate with or contradict the values we espouse in other areas, both individually and collectively. In other words, I begin with a rejection of the supposed neutrality of music implied by an approach that deals with music only as an empty sign for other things. Such an approach is possible only if one perversely refuses to engage with music on its own terms, as an internally elaborated and highly structured discourse.

A sociological inquiry into when and where a certain music becomes meaningful, and for whom, while valid and important, may tell us little about the music itself. One could imagine a sociological study of drugs proceeding along similar lines. But such a partial study would remain limited in its scope and application if it were not understood in relation to a medical analysis of the drugs in question and to an assessment of their physiological effects. Some might feel that the study would still be incomplete without a discussion of the problems and merits of different drugs and the ethical dimensions of the whole question of drug use. Such expectations do not apply in sociological studies of music use, because clearly one cannot talk objectively about the effects of music in any comparable way. Nevertheless, studies of musical meaning that completely ignore the music itself are clearly inadequate.

My approach here equally rejects the neutrality implied by the marketplace. Contemporary society may indeed be characterized by multiplicity and plurality, but the cultural products and positions that it throws up in bewildering proximity are not interchangeable choices and options, like so many different brands of a single product (music). We attach great importance to the sheer variety of music available to us, yet we lack even the most basic vocabulary for discussing when, how, and why different musics

can offer us genuinely different things. The paradox of music in a commercial context is that, for all the appearance of difference, musics that derive from quite different functions lose their distinctiveness because they
are assumed to serve the same function as all the others. Classical music is
shaped by different functional expectations than popular music, a fact all
but lost today because of the dominance of the functional expectations of
popular culture.

To argue that classical music, like art more generally, makes a claim to
types of functions and meanings distinct from those of popular culture is
to risk the charge of elitism. I address this question at several points, arguing that dominant uses of that term today, far from defending the idea of
democracy, undermine the most fundamental aspirations enshrined within
it. The charge of elitism should be leveled at those forces in society that hin-
der the development and opportunity of all of its members. So why is it
today so often the sign of entrenchment, a refusal of opportunity, a denial
of cultural or intellectual expressions of the aspiration that we might—
individually and collectively—realize our greater human potential?

This question is critical because it relates to a central claim of classical
music, one that distinguishes it from popular culture. Classical music, like
all art, has always been based on a paradoxical claim: that it relates to the
immediacy of everyday life but not immediately. That is to say, it takes aspects of our immediate experience and reworks them, reflecting them
back in altered form. In this way, it creates for itself a distance from the
everyday while preserving a relation to it. Talking about music and art,
which has always been a slightly suspect activity, becomes particularly suspect today because in attempting to highlight art's quality of separation
from the everyday, it refuses the popular demand that art should be as immediate as everything else. To insist on art's difference, its distance from
everyday life, comes dangerously close to an antipopulist position.

Art's critical attitude toward the everyday arouses suspicion not only
within popular culture but also within academic theory that deals with
popular culture. The influential theory of Pierre Bourdieu, for example, as
set out in his book *Distinction: A Social Critique of the Judgement of Taste*
(1979), has at its center the idea that cultural practices (from art and sport
to food and holidays) function entirely as sign systems for class distinctions
and that the idea of intrinsic aesthetic value or meaning is completely
bogus. The majority of recent writing on music and society, particularly
that which deals principally with popular culture, is written from a similar
sociological perspective. Its prime focus is empirical, and its concern is
with how music is actually used rather than how it may potentially be
used. Its concern with music as a social *practice* rather than as an aesthetic

text tends to displace questions of what music is (or might be) so that music comes to be defined solely in terms of its use.

My own approach owes more to the perspectives of philosophical aesthetics, on the one hand, and the practical concerns of musicians, on the other. I am concerned not with describing what *does* take place in the majority of cases but with arguing for what *could* take place, for a use of music to which we might aspire. My perspective is a critical one, opposed to an approach that too easily reinforces and legitimates "the way things are" simply by describing them. It argues against Bourdieu's reduction of aesthetic distinctions to vehicles of class distinctions by drawing a different conclusion from the same social facts. It suggests, on the contrary, that the class structure that presses art into its service is a reductive distortion of a collective aspiration that art itself encodes: the yearning to be more than we are. Art certainly relates to social use, but it is not defined by it. And while artworks are shaped by the social context in which they are generated, they remain resistant to a reductive, purely materialist reading.

Even the label "classical music" is problematic. The term implies a claim to universality, suggesting that such music transcends the judgments of any particular time or place. But the same claim underlines classical music's apparent lack of connection with the immediacy of everyday life, an aspect that ensures that it seems to be of little relevance for many people. It is a label so full of negative connotations that it might be better to avoid it altogether. But the arguments about classical music are somehow contained in its own awkward label, and it is perhaps more productive to wrestle with this than to reach for some neutral and sanitized alternative. Symptomatic of the difficulties here is the confusion about exactly which music the label refers to. Musicologists use it to refer only to the music of the late eighteenth and early nineteenth centuries (Haydn, Mozart, Beethoven). A more popular use has it denoting music from a wider historical period (say, from around 1600 to the present day) now associated with performance in a concert hall or opera house. More recently, commercial classical radio stations have used the term in a still broader way to include almost anything scored for orchestral or acoustic instruments, as opposed to the electrically amplified or generated sounds of popular music.

My own use of the term is quirky. I have no interest in reproducing the boundaries of a particular musical canon, whether it be the textbook list of great composers or the commercial charts of popular classics. Throughout this book, I use "classical music" simply to refer to music that functions *as art*, as opposed to entertainment or some other ancillary or background function. To try to define what distinguishes "music-as-art" from other functions of music, not just *which* music functions as art but *when* and *how* it does so, is the core of this study. Of course, to invoke the term "art" is merely to shift the problem into a wider arena, but in this way the discussion of musical value may at least take place in the context of ideas appropriate to it. The category of art, like that of God or religion, is perhaps so tainted by association with vacuous and pompous nonsense that we should really drop it without regret. But we have no other. To have no term with which to denote this type of object means we fail to recognize it at all.

Classical music today occupies a position similar to that of religion in other ways. For a majority of people, it derives from an earlier age, very different from our own, and survives only as an anachronism. While its apparent lack of modernity puts many people off, it is occasionally welcomed for the touch of solemnity and historical gravity it brings to big public occasions. It is tolerated so long as it presents itself as a wholly private matter—"a matter of faith"—but given little space if it begins to preach or make claims binding upon others. It has a place as one of many diverse cultural choices whose value is conferred by their use, by what they do for the people who use them rather than by any intrinsic properties. It is seen as a relatively closed world, defined by formal ritual and practices that divide it from the everyday. Classical music, like religion, thus survives in contemporary society shorn of the claims with which it was earlier identified.

If nothing else, its current legitimation crisis ought to engender a serious debate about musical value. To argue for what music might do for us, rather than endlessly exposing what it does not do, is to swim against the tide of intellectual fashion and to risk those cardinal sins of naïveté and being out of date. But, remarkably, today it seems necessary to point out that music may have a value that exceeds that conferred by its actual social use, if only to expose the narrowness of such definitions of value. My purpose here is not to salvage some lost crown for classical music or restore it to the pedestal from which it has been dislodged. It is rather to ask what it may still do for us and why such things may be important, and to suggest that if some of those important things are not offered elsewhere in our cultural life, the objective, social value of this music might yet be worth our attention.

"Value" is a key term in this book. Central to my argument is the distinction between the process by which value is conferred on music and a broader sense of values. The first has to do with signifying economies and social identity; the second is essentially an ethical question. The first is a question for a sociology of the way different people use different musics; the second is a concern for a critical and musically informed discussion of what the music itself proposes. Different musics are not neutral in terms of value systems; they are positioned because they quite literally *do* different things. And our participation in different musical systems necessarily involves us in these different value-positions that different musics construct. My suggestion is not only that we should be more self-aware of how different musics are positioned, but that we frequently identify with music whose value-position objectively contradicts that which we claim in other spheres of life—such as ethics, politics, or education.

Value becomes a relative idea today because it is everywhere turned into something quantifiable, as the principle of exchange value (i.e., price) is extended into all spheres of life. The value of anything becomes a shifting term in an economy of cultural meanings, defined by its relation to other signifying elements in the cultural system, not to anything "real" to which it might ultimately refer. Signifiers, as we are constantly told, are no longer tied to any concrete signifieds. The promise, on a British bank note, "to pay the bearer on demand ten pounds" is nowhere taken literally. Ten pounds of what? Of gold? We accept the conventionality of such references in every sphere of life, understanding that they make reference only to other elements in the system, not to some external standard.

Or do we? Don't we sometimes turn, exhausted, from the mind-numbing speed of our signifying economies with a sense of emptiness? Don't we feel uneasy about our own value in a world in which all values are relative? Don't we still pursue a quest, as old as humanity itself, to be valued on this earth, valued by others for being alive and valuing our consciousness of such a thing? And is that not a value that defies relativism and that has nothing to do with being a sign for something else? My claim is that music-as-art is shaped around this idea of value and that it claims a special status in our culture precisely because it invites us to participate in this sense of being valued in and for itself. It is not, fundamentally, a sign for something else—a cultural position, a style, a social status; it is a thing whose enactment makes possible the realization of a noncontingent sense of value.

To talk of art as cultural capital recalls the attitude that made the slave trade possible. People, too, can be made to be things and commodities, signs of economic status; but fundamental to our notion of humanity is the sense that who and what we are exceeds such misappropriation. We vehemently oppose such a reduction of what we consider to be inalienable and irreducible: the absolute value of the human spirit. Those who devalue art today point to the fact that only in the last few hundred years has our society privileged certain works and activities as art and promoted them to an almost sacred status. But it is no coincidence that this has taken place at the very time that the rationalization of human life—both private and public—has severely threatened the idea of individuals' value by making them dispensable units in a quantitative system. The high value accorded to art, classical music included, derives from its opposition to the social devaluation of the particular and individual. In a social world in which individuals become increasingly interchangeable and dispensable, art dwells on the particular and finds in it something of absolute value. In this way it redeems not just things but also people, whom society increasingly turns into things.

Music-as-art, at its best, is thus redemptive: it gives back to us a sense of our absolute value that a relativist society denies. It does so in a quite different way from the everyday means by which we attempt to bolster our fragile identities. Rather than serving us the moments of immediacy by which we affirm ourselves in everyday life, music-as-art requires us to enact a process, often discursive in nature, in which our everyday sense of self is at first not so much affirmed as loosened. The enactment of musical artworks requires a letting go of the immediacy that runs counter to the everyday. But its reward is that we are thus enabled to participate in a process which the everyday prevents: a self-unfolding of particularity that creates out of itself an objective whole. Music-as-art affirms our absolute value not by reflecting our "self" but by involving us in a process by which that self comes to understand itself more fully as a larger, trans-subjective identity. In this way the value of music-as-art is essentially ethical.

CHAPTER I. MUSICAL VALUES

A MATTER OF TASTE?

Perhaps nothing seems more futile than a dispute about music. To argue about the relative merits of different pieces of music appears as fatuous as arguing about the superiority of spring over autumn, or of red over blue. Common sense suggests that we should instead celebrate the differences and concede that individual preferences are never anything more than "a matter of taste." And indeed, the circular and vacuous nature of most arguments about music offers ample reason to avoid them.

Yet we do make such comparisons all the time. Our own musical preferences are shaped by judgments that, however unexpressed, impart greater value to some music than to other music. To consider some music "good" implies the possibility that other music might be less good, or even bad. Some people insist that their judgment is entirely personal and has no claim on anyone else, but others feel that their judgment has a wider validity, that some music simply *is* good and that its quality is more than a matter of individual opinion.

Whichever position we adopt, we make a similar assumption: that judgments about music are concerned with its quality and that its quality is related to its value. The more we value music, the more likely we are to defend its qualities against the opinion of others. And the more passionately we feel about the music we value, the more we feel that we are right and that our judgment is somehow objectively true, regardless of other people's opinions. But to voice such an opinion and to become involved in a dispute about musical quality proves to be frustrating and circular. The argument is irresolvable because, in the absence of any objective criteria, we either fall back on the subjective claims of "taste" and agree to differ or make ourselves ridiculous by stubbornly reasserting our own position.

Our frustration is deep-seated. It arises because music is *not* a purely personal matter: it is a shared, communal matter, even when we enjoy it alone. Music is communal property, made and played as a shared activity whether it is carried on by a solitary individual or a large group. The difference between the band performing at a huge open-air concert and the person who plays a guitar in the privacy of his or her bedroom is much less significant than it appears. The activity of making and listening to music involves us in something that is never merely personal. In this sense, music is like a language; when we "speak" or "listen" in musical language, we participate in a signifying system that is communally shared and defined, something that is larger than our own use of it and that we enter whenever we involve ourselves with music.

This linguistic aspect means that music is always more than "a matter of taste." We come into dispute with others about linguistic statements because they are more than personal. If someone asserts that the world is flat or that women are less intelligent than men, we are unlikely to shrug our shoulders and accept that, after all, "it's simply a matter of taste." Linguistic propositions are based on shared meanings; what they say is not endlessly deferred to some notion of subjective interpretation. Music partakes of an aspect of this. It does not (aside from its relation to words or images) make propositions about aspects of the real world, yet it "speaks" in ways that we find collectively meaningful.

The problem of making judgments about music is rooted here. Its collective, communal aspect suggests that its significance exceeds our purely individual responses, but at the same time we tend to experience music as significant in intensely personal and subjective ways. This seems to be an essential quality of music: it is collectively significant but speaks to the individual in a manner inaccessible to rational argument and dispute. While this twofold aspect is common to almost all musical experience, the way we understand it differs considerably in different societies and in different periods of our own history.

History makes it clear that there is nothing natural or essential about the ways we experience music today and the ways we account for that experience. Our fiercely emotive defense of our individual response to music (and our claim that this constitutes the sole criterion of its quality and significance) is not only of relatively recent historical origin but, from an anthropological perspective, is actually rather peculiar. The world's diverse musical cultures have been overwhelmingly communal activities, understood through collective frameworks such as religious and social rituals. This alone suggests that we might question some of our assumptions about music and the certainty with which we defend the absolute validity of our individual judgments.

Our position has an obviously democratic aspect: it accords equal rights and validity to the musical judgments of everyone. This position seems appropriate to a democratic society and, indeed, it was developed in tandem with the move to popular democracy. It is reinforced by a view of music with roots in the late eighteenth century and the beginnings of romanticism: the idea that music speaks *from* the individual directly *to* the individual and is a communication understood only "by the heart" and thus is not a matter for objective discussion or decision. The emphasis on individuality is evident both in the music of this period and in ideas about how we listen to it and the status of our personal experience. Romanticism's emphasis on an inward, emotional and essentially irrational experience thus provided the aesthetic legitimation for the individual's absolute authority in matters of musical judgment.

But musical judgments are never made in complete isolation. The formation of "taste cultures" has always been socially defined. Participation in certain genres of music—say, grand opera, street ballads, or rural folk music—was historically determined by a person's social position, not by a purely independent aesthetic choice. Indeed, from a sociological perspective, taste is always a social category rather than an aesthetic one; it refers to the way we use cultural judgments as social "currency," to mark our social positions. This may be less clear today, since contemporary society is characterized by the fragmentation of older taste cultures and the proliferation of new ones. In this context, cultural transactions take place with increasing rapidity—hence the heating up of the cultural economy and its rapid turnover of new products. Not only are taste cultures themselves shifting, but people now tend to move between them with greater ease. These factors contribute to a sense of the relativity of any single position. Contemporary musical choices are plural as never before, and the effect of that plurality is inevitably to confirm that, in matters of musical judgment, the individual can be the only authority.

This is in sharp contrast to the relatively minor status of individual "taste" in Western musical practice and aesthetics from the ancient Greeks until the late eighteenth century. To an earlier age, our contemporary idea of a complete relativism in musical judgment would have seemed nonsensical. One could no more make valid individual judgments about musical values than about science. Music was no more "a matter of taste" than was the orbit of the planets or the physiology of the human body. From Plato to Helmholtz, music was understood to be based on natural laws, and its value was derived from its capacity to frame and elaborate these laws in musical form. Its success was no more a matter of subjective judgment than the laws themselves.

The appeal to planetary motion as the foundation of musical harmony might seem faintly ludicrous to us now, but successive debates among musicians and theorists point to a single central precept: the power and significance that music holds for us derive from its relation to an order of things larger than ourselves. Today we might argue about whether that order is one "of nature" or whether it is not rather one "of society," of purely human making. But in both cases it concerns an order that confronts us, as individuals, as a reality over and against ourselves. The importance we accord to music is, in some way, derived from its ability to mediate our individual experience of that objective whole, whether it is conceived of as cosmic nature or human society. This is why music is irreducibly highly personal and subjective but also more than that—related to something that confronts us objectively, as the totality in which we live.

For us, the precise details of Greek or medieval theories may be unimportant. Their significance lies in the fact that they point to a constantly evolving debate about the nature, function, and value of music. The historical evolution of such theories demonstrates the importance of these questions to earlier societies. But, more broadly, it points to the importance of music in humankind's attempts to define an understanding of the world. If it now strikes us as amusing that music was once linked to astronomy or natural science, that is only because we fail to recognize *ourselves* there and the historical development of our *own* attempts to understand the world. If we no longer take music seriously as a way of defining our relation to the external world, perhaps we have become not more sophisticated but simply more self-absorbed.

Of course, there is an obvious contradiction in the fact that successive generations defended their ideas on music as derived "from nature," even as music and ideas about it changed radically. But this merely underlines the facts that social change is bound up with the changing idea of nature and that music is one of the ways society represents its own idea of the world to itself, one of the ways it renegotiates and reshapes that idea. The move from a medieval concern with outer nature (defined by natural science) to a more modern concern with inner nature (defined by psychology) does not alter the fact that music continues to be thought of as more than artificial. It is, certainly, a thing made by and for us—not something given in nature—but we continue to ascribe to it a more than purely formal or conventional force. It retains, for many in the contemporary world, the elemental force our predecessors attributed to its magical, mythical origins.

Debate about music, even technical debate between musicians, has always been an attempt to wrestle with this conundrum: music flows from individuals to other individuals and yet seems to be shaped by supra-individual forces. The basic model of that conundrum does not change whether it is understood in terms belonging primarily to magic, religion, mysticism, natural science, philosophy, psychology, sociology, or politics. This debate has an important ancillary presence to that of music itself, and its marginalization today should provoke some reflection. This discourse was a way of thinking not just about music, but about the way music mediated ideas of the world. It was thus a way of reflecting on our conceptions of the world, which is why musical theory was for centuries inseparable from theories of cosmology, natural science, and politics.

The lack of serious discourse on music today implies an absence of this self-reflection about music and its mediation of the ideas by which we live. This might give us some cause for concern. Argument about music has never delivered permanent answers; rather, its significance lay in its role within the continuous process of social change through a self-critique of cultural ideas. The absence of such musical debate today suggests a stasis underneath the rapid surface movement in contemporary culture. It also suggests an unquestioning acceptance of current musical practice and a passivity in relation to its products. This, in turn, suggests a certain lack of concern about music—a sign, perhaps, that music is not as important as it used to be even though it is far more ubiquitous. Argument, discourse, and debate point to things that are of importance, that wield power, that influence and impinge upon our lives. What doesn't matter to us, we never argue about.

This brings us back to our starting point: we don't argue about it because, after all, "it's all a matter of taste." To suggest otherwise today, to press for the validity of a musical judgment beyond personal preference is not only indecorous but somehow "politically incorrect"—it smacks of coercion and a kind of cultural high-handedness or elitism. But political correctness has little to do with a genuine political democracy that depends on the very kind of debate that is lacking here. It is, rather, the pseudo-democracy of a commercial culture that accords equal validity and equal status to all of its products. In the marketplace, all music becomes functionally equivalent, a fact elegantly realized in the uniformity of recorded music. The standard size, the standard box, and the standard price of CDs, lined up in their rows in the Virgin Megastore, reduce to functional equivalence music that originates from hundreds of regions of the world and from centuries of human history. The very multiplicity of these different musics has, ironically, contributed to the leveling of their functional differences.

The claim that individual taste is the sole criterion for musical judgment is suspect in the context of a marketplace whose logic it duplicates. One might at least pause to wonder why today's hits, apparently deeply significant to millions, become objects of derision in a matter of years.

This pattern bears a striking similarity to the requirements of commodity capitalism itself, which functions only by the constant renewal of its products. One might think that music, which doesn't wear out and is not strictly a thing at all, would serve this system rather poorly. But music today is thought of almost entirely in terms of a recorded object (the CD), itself the result of a long process of commodification that goes back at least to the production of sheet music for domestic use at the end of the eighteenth century. But neither sheet music nor recordings wear out quickly enough for the market's demands. Turning music into an object, and thus into a commodity, was nothing compared to the accelerating process of its own redundancy. The production of the "new," on which capitalism's infinite cycle is based, came to be a demand in musical composition during the same period, signaling a complex relationship between musical aesthetics and commodity capitalism that remains with us today.

The music industry's demand for a rapid turnover of products and the formation of contemporary taste cultures are mutually dependent. In this context, music becomes one element in a broader tide of cultural fashion where the products themselves count for less than their function as a sign for the contemporary and for a particular position within the contemporary. Music thus becomes like clothing fashion or interior design: we might feel strongly about it at the time and even buy the journalistic commentary that explains why it reflects the spirit of our age, but we are able to distance ourselves from it only a few months later because its principal function, as a sign for a particular present, is more important than its intrinsic qualities.

In this context, the objection that "it's all a matter of taste" takes on a rather different aspect. Our musical choices are rarely the wholly free and independent actions of a sovereign individuality, surveying the products of world music from on high. They are more often our responses to the continual demands to select from a changing but always determined musical choice. This process appears to have an attractiveness which goes beyond that of the music itself and for which, in some ways, the music may serve only as a symbol. Just as the process of commodity culture requires that we buy, our own identity is confirmed and enhanced by our participation in that process. Investing in the products of the music industry is one way we define our personal identities. Not to do so is, in many ways, eccentric and exposes one to marginalization in a society defined above all by the requirement to be up to date. This identification process is often profound and intense: the line "it's all a matter of taste" also has a defensive function, because a challenge to the music through which one identifies oneself is experienced with the same anxiety as a personal attack.

The logic of the marketplace validates its products by the very act of selling and buying. That the object is for sale implies that it is valuable; its purchase confirms its value. Although musical objects have an equivalent exchange value (all CDs cost about the same), the cultural value of different musics is clearly differentiated by the quantitative logic of the market. The chart system is the modern answer to the debates of Greek philosophers and medieval scholars: if the act of buying confirms the value of the musical object, then the greater the number of the same object sold, the more valuable it must be. The sleight of hand that elides musical or cultural value with economic value is not mine; it is effected by the market itself. It is a self-confirming process. Music sells because it is popular. It is popular because it has sold.

We should perhaps question the way musical value has been reduced to a one-dimensional commercial definition. What does it mean, in this context, to question the musical value of a piece that has sold millions of copies and topped charts for weeks? Its commercial value speaks for itself and is confirmed by the symbolic award of gold and platinum discs. But what does it mean to suggest that its musical value is not necessarily equivalent to its commercial value? We are approaching a situation where the question is simply meaningless. And of those who might acknowledge the question, more and more might feel that it is irrelevant. The sheer presence of this music confirms its own validity. The reverse may well be the case, too: it becomes equally meaningless or irrelevant to assert the musical value of work that appears to have no commercial value. In reply to the assertion that this music is good comes the question, "Good for whom?" Its lack of commercial success, following this logic, is de facto proof that it is effectively good for nobody: it has zero value.

The terms in which we might debate this claim seem to be absent—hence the regression of aesthetic discussion into circularity and vacuity. The same brief "debate" takes place with tiresome regularity: A says this music is great and deserves to be heard; B asks why, if it is so great, nobody else seems to want to hear it. A replies that the commercialization of music has stunted people's ability to listen to challenging music. B feels insulted, suggests that A is an elitist, and goes on to ask what makes this music so important anyway. A shrugs petulantly, saying that it is quite obviously "great music" and that if B is unable to hear that for himself then that is a sign of how philistine this country has become. The discussion ends with A and B talking over each other.

Parody aside, the absence of any real terms for such a debate characterizes contemporary arguments over state funding and public subsidy of the arts, a subject that deserves a more informed and articulate discussion. The whole topic has become a tired one precisely because it seems locked into the same superficial and circular pattern. The burden of proof falls on those who want to assert the aesthetic value of music that does not seem to have sufficient commercial value to survive without some intervention in market economics. But the evidence for this aesthetic value is elusive and the case usually relies upon vague appeals to "artistic greatness" and "cultural heritage." This may have worked for a while because often those who made private donations or granted public subsidies also held this view. But it may not always be so, and others would find rather shocking the implication that certain kinds of music are so important that they should be supported at the public's expense, even though they are enjoyed by a very small and often wealthy minority. Even more shocking perhaps, if not offensive, is the implication that some music is greater than other music—that it is, in musical terms, *more* valuable even in the face of a completely opposite commercial valuation.

This offends against the pseudo-democracy that the market seems to promise because it implies that the musical judgment of a minority is, in this case, keener than that of a majority. It undermines the illusion that the act of buying implies, that commercial value and aesthetic value are equivalent. But only at this stage might a real debate begin, as one begins to ask what a musical judgment might be in the face of a commercial one, who and on what grounds makes such a judgment, and what the validity of that judgment is in the face of others.

A DEMOCRATIC CULTURE?

These are practical questions, not merely theoretical ones. Publicly funded cultural institutions—like the Arts Council in the United Kingdom or the National Endowment for the Arts in the United States—have been shaped by a single dominant assumption: that "great" art and music are intrinsically valuable and should be kept alive by a combination of state subsidy and corporate sponsorship if they become commercially nonviable in the open marketplace. The argument is that everyone in a modern democracy should have equal access to the benefits of art and music, both that of our own time and that of our "cultural heritage." The mission statement of the National Endowment for the Arts is typical: "The arts reflect the past, enrich the present, and imagine the future. The National Endowment for the Arts, an investment in America's living cultural heritage, serves the public good by *nurturing* the expression of human creativity, *supporting* the cultivation of community spirit, and *fostering* the recognition and appreciation of the *excellence* and *diversity* of our nation's artistic accomplishments" (NEA Web site, accessed September 2001).

The language of parental care displaces any debate about the value of what is being nurtured, supported, and fostered: art, like a child, is inherently valuable and in need of such solicitude. Statements like this are equally vague about precisely what is being supported—hence the use of broad terms like "cultural heritage," "public good," "human creativity," and "community spirit." The possibility that "excellence" might imply an undemocratic exclusivity is offset by the parallel concern with "diversity." Few people would object to such wholesome and all-embracing aims, and, indeed, the NEA proudly cites a 1996 Lou Harris poll finding that Americans support a government-funded arts program by a majority of three to one, with 61 percent saying they would be willing to each pay five dollars more per year in taxes to fund the arts (NEA Web site, accessed September 2001).

The practical reality of state funding for the arts is, of course, far more contested. While a broad section of the population may support the principle of fostering creativity, there is far less agreement about which actual projects, events, objects, buildings, or artists should be funded. When a city's carnival has its funding cut at the same time that the subsidy for its opera house is increased, the issues surrounding the judgment of cultural value become political. In Britain, government intervention in culture has been handled, since 1997, by the Department of Culture, Media, and Sport, an eclectic grouping of disparate areas designed, one assumes, to smooth over awkward questions about the relative values and functions of quite different cultural activities. Symptomatic of that, perhaps, is the department's tendency to talk about "the creative industries," a group of activities worth over £60 billion per year to Britain, and activities in which performing, visual, and plastic arts rub shoulders with commercial film and music, architecture, design, publishing, broadcasting, multimedia, and fashion. Only by restricting the idea of value to financial considerations could these unrelated areas be considered together. In every other respect, the criteria for, say, the value of a new orchestral work by a contemporary composer and the criteria for a new computer game are not only different but probably antithetical.

Beneath the generic language and uncontroversial "good causes" that government bodies seek to support lies a political minefield. As soon as one turns to specifics, it is obvious that, financial resources being finite, support for one thing means neglect of another. Whereas disagreement between individuals on a matter of taste may be inconsequential, at the level of public funding it becomes clear that cultural judgments have to do with real social and political power. The aim of a genuine cultural democracy seems noble: as British Culture Secretary Chris Smith put it, an arts policy aims "to make the best things in life available to the greatest number." But it runs into problems when one stops to ask *who* it is that decides which are "the best things" and *what* about them is so valuable that everyone should need them.

These questions were brought to the fore during the 1970s by a range of groups, all of whom challenged the fundamental assumptions of the "cultural democracy" ideal pursued by state funding programs. Grassroots activists and community artists found unlikely allies in a generation of academics and cultural theorists disputing the universal value of the "great tradition," the canon of works that public programs continued to present as the cultural heritage of the entire population. So while the policies of bodies like Britain's Arts Council, designed to improve access to the arts, *seemed* harmless enough, the council was increasingly challenged to explain what was so important about the traditional arts that people should be encouraged to participate in them. Who decided which artworks were important and on what authority did they now press them on those who had so far managed perfectly well without them? From this perspective, state arts funding was seen as an essentially patriarchal, top-down system in which the art of a small, affluent, and well-educated minority was being advanced as having universal greatness and importance. For those in control of public funds to talk of the unrealized "cultural needs" of people (as distinct from what the people themselves wanted) was seen as high-handed at the very least. A modern, multicultural society had no place for this kind of nineteenth-century cultural paternalism: instead of the cultural democracy cherished by groups like the Arts Council, such countermovements proposed a more radical democratization of culture.

This was a significant moment in the history of state cultural policy. For so long, the greatness of high art and classical music had been taken for granted. In an earlier, aristocratic society, a lack of understanding or appreciation of art was considered proof of the lower classes' inferior sensibilities and intelligence. In a more enlightened and democratic age, this lack of appreciation was believed to show an educational deprivation that bodies like the Arts Council or the NEA and a host of educational outreach programs continue to try to redress. But the challenge thrown down by calls for the democratization of culture was quite different: it questioned the fundamental assumptions of the canon, assumptions about the inherent greatness of certain artists and works, and about their claims to significance for all people in all times.

Central to this challenge was its focus on the creativity of "ordinary" people and the value of creative activity as an expressive tool for both the individual and the community. This shift of focus from great artists to ordinary people, from the passive contemplation of other people's works to the active participation in one's own projects, was a key characteristic of the local resistance to state-imposed policies. In Britain, this argument goes back to the origins of the Arts Council during World War II, when those involved in stimulating amateur work resisted the tendency to withdraw funding in order to concentrate it on maintaining the excellence of professional productions. Today, a policy of practical, hands-on music education continues to argue that if adequate resources are not allocated to its activities, there will soon be no audience left for the "excellent performances" to which the greater part of the public music subsidy has traditionally been directed.

The shift of attention from great works to ordinary people entailed, if not devaluing great works, certainly displacing them from their hitherto central and elevated position. Starting with people rather than works meant starting from the individual's specific cultural identity and social context which often had little to do with the traditions of classical art and music. There were compelling and self-evident reasons for this in terms of the multicultural nature of modern societies, particularly of metropolitan societies. But the shift was also accompanied by a more general assertion of the equal validity of popular creative forms, as compared with those of high art. It was not so much high art itself that was opposed but, rather, the assumption that it carried a greater value than other forms. For many, high art was simply the cultural tradition of a nineteenth-century bourgeoisie and had no claim on those whose lives and perspectives were quite different. From this position, the overwhelming tendency of state funding to favor "high" or bourgeois art showed an indefensible political bias toward the tastes of the middle classes.

For most people, however, the topic hardly requires discussion or argument. Outside of debates about funding, the specific claims of high art and classical music are simply not heard in contemporary culture and indeed are hardly voiced anymore. Classical music is not consciously rejected; it is simply one cultural option among many that an individual chooses not to take up. But it is symptomatic of a profound shift in attitudes toward high art that such arguments have increasingly become part of academic discussion. Musicology has often been slow to respond to developments in cultural theory because, more than other disciplines in the humanities, its approach has been characterized by the same degree of autonomy apparently exhibited by its subject matter. Music's often-cited "abstract" quality has thus tended to insulate musicology from broader social questions to a degree not possible in the study of visual or literary art. But in the last decade or so, this has been powerfully challenged from a number of different directions, including ethnomusicology, popular music studies, and feminist musicology.

Until very recently, issues of race, class, and gender simply were not deemed relevant to classical music, which was considered a nonreferential art form whose value lay precisely in the transcendence of such worldly differences. That music is as involved in the historical and material realities of the social world as any other cultural form has now become the focus of much important work. This starts from the assumption that musical works are not value-free; even when they have no words and refer to no obvious external things, they adopt certain positions and perspectives that are fundamentally social in character. Such studies challenge the formation of the canon itself—that group of works which are accorded the accolade of being "timelessly great" and are thus the basis of the classical music industry and the curriculum of traditional music education. Historically, art has been the preserve of those with social power, and the selection of certain works to form the canon of great art is itself an activity of that elite. As such, the canon may well be that body of work selected (deliberately or not) because it was the aesthetic embodiment and sign of those in power. Art literally represented power, wealth, and domination, and as a medium it stood for everything that was highly cultivated, unique, refined, and valuable. In short, it served as a sign for the elitism of those in power—those for whom art was made. Aesthetics and its claim to universal values is, from this perspective, simply a mystification of the material reality.

For these reasons, recent thinking on music often exhibits a grave distrust or even guilt about the corpus of music we have inherited. On the one hand it is presented as one of the greatest achievements of the Western mind, but on the other it may betray its origins in social privilege and exclusion. This might seem extreme, but it forms part of a noticeable distancing of the establishment from its earlier identification with high art. When politicians appear on a platform with pop singers, their motives may be blatantly populist, but so, too, is their marked avoidance of public appearances with representatives of an art world considered too minority, too serious, and too highbrow. Whereas the nineteenth-century middle classes aspired to an upward cultural mobility by taking part in activities formally reserved for the aristocracy (like classical music recitals), the tendency of the much larger middle class toward the end of the twentieth century was to a *downward* cultural mobility. In the politics of contemporary cultural style, classical music has an increasingly negative status. It's not just "uncool," but comes to be politically suspect, associated not only with a parental generation but with the tastes of an elitist social group (well-off and well-educated) whose patronage of classical music is perceived as a gesture of class distinction—in short, snobbery. This is why it is not only a younger generation that distances itself today from classical music but, increasingly, the whole of a middle class that was historically its driving force. The aspiration toward social advancement through economic wealth remains unchanged, but it is often accompanied by musical choices that, in their sanitized versions of popular culture, reflect a desire to avoid the pretentious overtones of high art. Even classical musicians now feel the need to demonstrate their popular credentials by appearing on the same platform as pop musicians or producing versions of classical music that supposedly bridge the gap between the two worlds.

Amid the proliferation of musical choices, the traditional legitimation for the classical canon either comes under close scrutiny or, more often, simply dissolves and vanishes. In the past, classical music made an implicit claim to aesthetic and even moral superiority over other musics. The legacy of that claim still underwrites the centrality of classical music in educational curricula and in government funding policy for the arts, a position that is of course disproportionate to the amount of public interest in classical music. But for the first time, this claim is challenged, not only from *without* (by classical music having to take its place alongside every other musical commodity in an expanding market) but also from *within* (by the questioning of basic assumptions of musical value by parts of the academic establishment, as well as by those who market and promote music).

The extension of musical choices is thus simultaneous with the erosion of older discourses by which music used to be evaluated. Classical music not only has to jostle for position like any other in the free market of an open, commercial "culture industry"; it has to do so without the framing social rituals and academic legitimation that shored up its former status. Where it has adapted to the new technological and commercial world, it has achieved some startling successes. In Britain, the commercial radio station Classic FM reached an audience of over 6 million listeners within a few years of its launch, dwarfing the audience for Radio 3, the BBC's longstanding classical music station. Increasingly, the marketing of classical music performers and recordings has adopted the approaches developed in popular music. The music's inherent quality is no longer relied on to speak for itself; its promotion is based on what is promised by the performer and the subliminal message of its packaging.

Without a doubt, the loosening of classical music from some of the social trappings that surrounded it in the nineteenth century has been refreshing. Many people were put off classical music by the perception that it was guarded by a pretentious and stuffy layer of social ritual almost designed to repel the uninitiated. Showing that the music itself has quite different and immediate qualities has been one of the most welcome benefits of a more recent context for classical music. But this has come at a price that the market exacts from everything it sells: music becomes functionally equivalent, and its value is conferred by the buyer, not by the music itself.

The concept of art, on which the distinctive claims of classical music are based, ceases to be meaningful in this context. First, the idea of art proposes a particular class of objects that assume a different function to everyday things; second, the idea of art claims a value that is not contingent on the perception of any particular individual. Such claims are easily drowned out in a society characterized by a complete relativism of cultural judgments. Everything is art in this context—gardening, cookery, home decorating, sport, sex. At the same time, nothing is art, in the sense that, for many people, art makes no legitimate claim over anything else. Judgments about art and music become individual, shaped by local rather than universal criteria, reflecting our participation in certain cultural and social groups. This relativity of cultural judgments seems like a logical and necessary consequence of democratic principles. But the absence of shared criteria and a consequent value relativism is neither equivalent to democracy nor necessarily compatible with it. Culture, in the broadest sense, is inseparable from the areas of life that we think of as social and political. Our ability to make judgments about the world and to form opinions on social and personal issues is shaped by the cultural forms through which we experience the world—which, in many ways, *are* our world. Cultural tradition, some would argue, has an important role to play in contemporary society as a counterweight to what is merely fashion or fad, a society in which media construction of public opinion is too often a substitute for genuine debate and independent thought.

These debates are not new. What *is* relatively new is the fact that they have been all but silenced by the constant and noisy demands of the everyday—something from which debate, by definition, has to step back a few paces. But, where they are heard at all, the arguments over classical music point to a fundamental contradiction about art that, in turn, points to a larger contradiction about the nature of democracy. The impulse that motivates public arts policies is primarily democratic: to give universal access to what are deemed unique cultural practices and objects. But these practices and objects are often inaccessible in a deeper sense, even when entrance to the gallery or the concert is free. The most highly valued works of art, especially in the case of modern and recent work, are often prized precisely because of their high degree of sophistication within a particular tradition, something that tends to prevent such works from being immediately understood or enjoyed by a general public. This points to an apparently undemocratic aspect of art itself: it resists and partly opposes commonsense immediacy. It is not immediately graspable because, as art, it distinguishes itself by being different from the everyday world, a world that it transforms rather than reproduces. It often requires effort, time, and a process that, while having little to do with school or college, is essentially educative.

This paradox goes to the heart of democracy, and every public arts policy has to wrestle with it. Political democracy has always been a more complex proposition than that implied by universal suffrage. The principle of "one person, one vote" does not guarantee the absolute sovereignty of the individual. It accords the individual an equal right to exercise a judgment and to choose, but only regarding which legislative body one will entrust with making virtually every other judgment about the organization of public life. In reality, democratically elected governments constantly make decisions that, if taken as individual issues, a majority of the population might not vote for. In its place, our society is characterized by the extension of the voting system into completely inappropriate and irrelevant areas: we are constantly being invited to phone in to register our vote for the best goal of the tournament, the best song of the competition, or our favorite poem. The old panel of experts is displaced by an automated telephone system recording the votes of the nation. The best goal, song, or poem is simply the one with the most votes. What could be more democratic?

The judgment of value by any other means is, it seems, less than democratic—a situation that makes the whole idea of expertise implicitly elitist. Though we still believe in that notion when applied to medicine and science, it is increasingly irrelevant in questions of art or culture. Here, experts are irrelevant for the simple reason that the sole criterion for judging something like music is personal pleasure, a realm where the judgment of experts has no authority. Those shaping state policies on the arts thus find themselves caught between two conflicting ideas of art. On the one hand, art is not separated from the rest of contemporary cultural practice and is judged by the same criteria of pleasure, fashion, and the demarcation of social space. On the other, certain kinds of art and music are claimed to be valuable *despite* their low estimation in popular judgment.

The impossible task of a government arts body is thus to reconcile two conflicting ideas of democracy: the idea, enshrined in the marketplace, that the customer's right to choose is unassailable, and the idea, enshrined in national institutions like legal or educational systems, that asserts a claim on all individuals, whatever their personal tastes or preferences. If the arts body tends too far to the first position, it is accused of failing to protect the rights of minorities against the tyranny of the market-led majority and failing to provide cultural choices to those traditionally denied access to high culture. If it tends too far to the second, it is accused of paternalistically prescribing the nation's cultural diet and foisting the tastes of a well-educated elite on the majority, which does not share those tastes.

At the heart of this dilemma is the idea that democracy needs protection against itself. This has often seemed rather shocking as a basis for a cultural theory—as it is in the work of critics like T. S. Eliot, Allan Bloom, or T. W. Adorno. But its basic assumption, that people make choices which may contradict their objective interests, is no less that of policy-making in democratic administrations. Whether controlling inflation through raising interest rates or policing traffic laws, democratic governments frequently limit our individual freedoms in the broader interests of the whole and thereby, indirectly, of ourselves. If I drive too fast in a built-up area, I am opposed by a law that restricts my freedom in the name of defending other people's right not to be killed by a speeding motorist. In doing so, it protects my own right not to be killed by another speeding motorist.

We broadly accept government legislation restricting the use of alcohol, drugs, firearms, and pornography. We subscribe to laws that limit our freedom to change our environment or our freedom to behave in certain ways in public. Many of these laws are inseparable from a moral position that may be contentious even as it continues to be the basis of a law that makes a claim on everyone. The law, like the moral imperative, has as its justification its claim to protect us not only from other people but also from ourselves. The idea of law, from its theological origins onward, implies that we aspire to be something greater than we are. Like education, law is based on a *transcendental* premise: it promises something that exceeds the present reality of its participant, denying an immediate gratification in return for a greater reward later. Living in a democracy constantly demands our compliance with the same principle: my not violating a no-parking zone today ensures (via everyone else's compliance) that I can travel freely down this road every day. But the pseudo-democracy of the marketplace is based on an *empirical* premise: it delivers something immediate and tangible. It promises to satisfy instantly the demands it creates, and it accords to every individual the absolute right to have their demands satisfied—a democratic right whose hollowness is self-evident given the disparity between individuals' financial resources. The right to exercise choice, the judgment of value, and the sovereignty of the individual are all mutually confirmed in the act of buying. Nothing would cause a greater affront to the popular notion of democracy than a restriction of what one could buy.

But this pseudo-democracy is based on a paradox. If the judgments we make in a free marketplace are constitutive of our individuality, the value of that individuality is undermined if all judgments are equally valid. This paradox points to a deeper contradiction at the heart of modern life. Our conception of ourselves and of our society is predicated on our inalienable individuality and on our rights as individuals. Definitive of that individuality is our capacity for independent thought and hence our right to make our own judgments about the world. These judgments are devalued in a social context in which any idea of an objective judgment has become impossible. In making judgments, we lay claim to the possibility of an objective judgment even though we may agree that our own falls short of it. But the value of our judgments is conferred by the possibility of that goal. To deny the possibility of that objective judgment is not only to devalue the judgments of individuals but also to devalue the notion of individuals themselves, who by the same token become merely contingent, arbitrary positions in a shifting, utterly relative game.

It is a paradox, then, that while we insist on the sovereignty of individual choice in all that we do and buy as fundamental to our idea of democracy, we have all but expunged the claims of judgment as such. It is symptomatic of our politically correct sensitivities that the idea of choice has almost replaced the idea of discrimination, a word that has entirely negative connotations today. To be discriminating used to mean to be capable of exercising judgment—to be wise, in fact. It implied that one understood the world and could discern the difference between things. We can hardly use "discrimination" in this way anymore, because the idea of discrimination is now inextricably linked to the idea of rejection and exclusion (whether on racial, sexual, or other grounds). We now use the word in the sense of "to discriminate against" rather than "to discriminate between." But not to be discriminating, in the sense of not seeing the difference between things, is the mark of a pseudo-democracy. And that pseudo-democracy is built not on mutual respect but on a lack of respect for one another and even for ourselves. Because discrimination (being aware of the difference between things) is a corollary of our fundamental insistence on our own individuality and that of others, recognition of difference is a confirmation of human individuality, of the inviolable identity of every one of us.

WHO NEEDS CLASSICAL MUSIC?

Perhaps this assessment of the status of classical music today seems un-necessarily pessimistic. There is, after all, evidence to suggest that classical music, far from suffering a demise, has in recent years enjoyed a marked in-crease in popularity. But the limited degree of commercial success in some areas of classical music has come at a price: the loss of the distinctive claim made for classical music as a whole. The newfound popularity of some classical music depends on it dropping a claim that is at odds with pop-ulism and the logic of commercialism. The claim is based on an under-standing of music as defined primarily by the musical work and its inward, intrinsic, and objective properties, and only secondarily in terms of listen-ers' responses to it. This emphasis has little place in commercial music, whose success, by definition, rests on being shaped by commercial de-mands, not purely musical ones. Classical music does not ignore its listen-ers' desires, but it is shaped by its adherence to internal, musical demands that are often at odds with the pleasurable immediacy commercial success requires.

Of course, classical music can be, and frequently is, approached in this way, in which case it functions more or less successfully as another kind of commercial music. The kind of classical music that flourishes in this envi-ronment is that which is adaptable to the dominant functions of commer-cial music; other kinds of classical music, such as contemporary music and much chamber music, are often far less adaptable and tend to be excluded. The commercial success, over the last decade, of nineteenth-century Ital-ian opera arias or baroque concertos derives from their use in quite differ-ent contexts than the traditional ones of classical music. The longer tradi-tion of "easy listening" to which their popularity relates is more accurately thought of as a kind of popular music. One might say that popular music, defined as a set of musical uses and functions rather than a musical style, has broadened its ambit to include musical styles previously considered classical. The music hasn't changed, of course, but the way it is used and the value system that underwrites it may well have done.

The legitimation crisis of classical music thus arises from a mismatch between the manner in which it becomes meaningful as art and the domi-nant context of musical culture—that is to say, popular culture. The dis-cursive and formal concerns of classical music are out of place in a context where immediacy is a central criterion. In this context, only those classical works that exhibit a greater degree of immediacy will be successful, a suc-cess bought at the price of backgrounding their other characteristics. Clas-sical music and popular music differ in this important respect. To point out this difference is not to denigrate either tradition but to criticize the increasing uniformity and one-dimensional character of contemporary musical *practice*. Musical practice today reinforces the false assumption on which it is based—that all musics fulfill the same function and can be meaningfully judged by the same criteria.

In this context, the distinctive claims of classical music are generally not heard. They are mostly no longer voiced, and when they are, they increasingly tend to sound hollow. On the whole, therefore, these claims have not been directly challenged. There has been no public examination of classical music and a requirement that it justify the special status it used to claim. Rather, the world has simply changed around it beyond all recognition and, to a large degree, has left it marginalized. Today classical music increasingly resembles a curio preserved from an earlier age, as if orchestra members who had been playing in an empty concert hall for the past fifty years had finally wandered outside to find themselves in the middle of a vast cosmopolitan city like New York, time-travelers who not only didn't recognize this busy, loud, hectic, crisscrossing world but were themselves invisible to it.

For those involved in classical music today, this feeling of bemusement is not uncommon. The marginalization of the classical canon in dominant media channels has been swift, and the displacement of its value has left classical music curiously exposed. The challenges it faces are serious, not least because classical music so easily serves as a sign for wealth, privilege, and social distinction. Since it is marginalized, in part, because of these functions, we must ask whether it has, in spite of them, some remainder that exceeds them. In other words, does classical music offer a level of meaning that is not entirely negated by such (ab)use? Can it claim to be valuable in a way not determined by its social origins and its social fate, or do "great works" simply evaporate once one has expunged this element of social signaling and class distinction? If that were the case, is a sociology of culture correct in suggesting that what is claimed as aesthetic value is no more than the value which works have accrued as tokens of social relations?

These questions should inform significant debate about classical music today, but they are strikingly absent in the few arenas where their distinctive claims are still assumed and thus contested—in debates about public subsidy and education. It is here that the legitimation crisis is perhaps most keenly felt and the lack of cogent arguments and understanding most obviously exposed. Classical music draws on such a long and entrenched tradition of distinction that now, suddenly challenged, it finds itself hopelessly tongue-tied. It blusters, gets frustrated and petulant, and is too often inclined to turn away with that air of superciliousness that, for many of its detractors, had characterized it all along. But there is another side—a classical music that is shy of stating its own case. This side is apt to retreat in the face of its public rejection, locking the music room door behind itself (as perhaps many composers have done). But if the distinctive claim of classical music is to be heard, it must voice itself. Classical music needs to say what it does, why it might be important, why it might be necessary, why perhaps society should pay for it even when it is not popular. Most of all it needs to turn the question around and ask society why it is *not* popular. What is it about classical music that we don't like? What is it that we reject in classical music, and what does an entertainment culture give us that matters so much more to us? In the end, what *does* matter to us?

Unless we address these questions, important arguments in arts education and funding will continue to reproduce the assumptions of entrenched positions. When such arguments surface in the media, they rarely receive more than one-dimensional treatment. Amid all the public rows surrounding the closing and refurbishing of the Royal Opera House in London in 1997, it was hard to find a balanced discussion of why an opera house might be worth paying for with public money. The classical music establishment does itself no favors by dismissing such a question as "philistine." It deserves an answer, one that might help to bridge the gap between the minority, who see it as self-evident, and the majority, who find it hard to see the slightest justification for such huge public expense.

The case against it is simple. If we wanted to hear international opera singers in lavish new productions or complex contemporary music requiring hours of extra rehearsal, we would pay for it. We would pay for it the same way we pay when we want to eat in a restaurant or buy new clothes. That not enough of us are willing to pay the real, unsubsidized cost of hearing opera or contemporary music is proof, runs this argument, that collectively we don't want it enough. We make other choices instead—for restaurants and clothes, or for CDs we can listen to at home. It is not, economists would argue, that we no longer value things other than financially, but simply that those other ways of valuing are all translatable into hard economic terms. In other words, what we value we will pay for; and if we won't pay for it, we don't value it. Not enough of us, it seems, value live and innovative opera productions or contemporary music sufficiently to pay for them to operate without state subsidy.

Yet as long as we continue to pay taxes to central and local government, we collectively endorse the idea that democracy and individual consumer choice are not synonymous. If funding of public institutions and services were left to voluntary individual contributions, few would survive. Instead, we largely put aside our personal preferences and assent (by paying taxes) to a collective contract. In this way we support not just hospitals, emergency services, the armed forces, and the judiciary but also schools, universities, museums, libraries, art galleries, theaters, and concert halls. Our collective support for this public funding is predicated on the idea that it will guarantee the quality and wide accessibility of those services that we deem to be of particular importance.

For many, however, it seems increasingly inappropriate that music and the arts should be a matter of state concern or subsidy. One of the results of music becoming commodified into a thing, rather than an activity, is its appropriation as a personal possession. Far from being a matter of public provision (like education or hospitals), music is more often considered a sign and tool of private, inward space. So while national and local government still considers art a social amenity, alongside public parks, libraries, and swimming pools, individually we tend to think of music as a private leisure activity that we are happy to pay for as we would pay for a meal, furniture, or clothes. By the same token, we may be equally unwilling to contribute to the cost of such personal items for other people.

The arguments that traditionally legitimate public funding are rarely heard today. In some areas, such as education, they continue to command a general assent: the vast majority of us consent to a compulsory education system for five- to sixteen-year-olds, both by paying for it through taxes and by sending our children to school. We do so because we are more or less convinced by the legitimating argument surrounding education. Although the requirements of subsequent adult employment may be at the forefront here, much that is central to educational practice can only be explained by older and larger systems of legitimation, a philosophy of education that talks of rounded individuals and a developed awareness of the world, ourselves, and each other. In other words, we collectively subscribe to the idea that a modern democracy requires its members to be educated, literate, and numerate individuals with a sense of critical argument, rational thought, and developed awareness on a range of social, political, ethical, and technological issues. Moreover, this idea includes the sense that this is not just necessary but desirable for the individual, that education helps realize the full potential of each of us.

It is in the context of this broad, humanist aspiration that classical music has traditionally understood itself. In the eighteenth and nineteenth centuries, classical music developed alongside a philosophical discourse that legitimated music not as entertainment but as a form of self-expression and knowledge. On the basis of this claim, to be part of the broader Enlightenment project of human self-development, classical music has sought to differentiate itself from a purely entertainment function. The "great works" within this tradition, it has always been implied, derive their specific value from the particularly acute or powerful way in which they embody the key ideals of that Enlightenment humanism—that is to say, ideas of individuality, freedom, and self-identity expressed in a collective whole.

From this broader perspective, one can begin to answer substantive questions, such as why it might be right for an opera house to be subsidized by public money. The defense of this privileged status of classical music hinges on the idea that it is more than "just entertainment." In the past it has existed alongside an elaborate discourse about what constitutes that something *more*—or, at the very least, *different*. That difference used to be signaled by the term "art," but that is no longer a meaningful distinction for most people, being an institutional label rather than a substantive one. In some circles, it continues to have a certain weight, and patrons of the arts, whether private individuals, corporate sponsors, or public institutions, are often content to support or purchase "art" without being too worried about the nature of the art itself or who makes such judgments for them. But this is becoming increasingly suspect, both with funding bodies and media commentators who want more hard-edged facts, and with academics and educational policy makers who take a more pluralist and historically informed view on questions of universality.

There is an urgent need for an understanding of what music may be and what it may potentially do. To invoke older ideas associated with classical music may seem rather grand and pompous to contemporary ears, but perhaps no more so than the ideas on which education itself is legitimated. That recalling older and grander ideas should strike an odd note is perhaps itself proof of how one-dimensional contemporary musical practice has become. Different musical traditions may well be available as never before, but their aesthetic and functional differences are paradoxically neutralized as never before. The logic of commodity capitalism forces every cultural practice to account for itself according to the same universal commercial criteria. So whereas classical music used to be underwritten by claims of intellectual or spiritual content, today it is far more likely to be legitimated by claims of its new popularity and thus commercial value. The older claims, based on Enlightenment ideals of freedom, self-expression, and genius, are preserved as a veneer but are increasingly seen as insufficient justification in themselves.

Despite all that, the legitimation crisis classical music faces has some potential benefits. It arises in part from a characteristic of classical music itself, that its own concern with autonomous formal processes and degree of abstraction from the everyday tends toward an introverted and insulated isolation from social reality. The condition of its freedom for aesthetic elaboration is also the means by which it can become mere aestheticism, a sophisticated escapism. As a social practice, classical music's round of concerts and recitals and opera performances can appear to be no more than the attributes of rich living (like horse racing or expensive restaurants) and to bear no relation to the high ideals of romantic aesthetics. Classical music may well have grown smug, and its current legitimation crisis, for all its seriousness, offers a fragile opportunity for a rejuvenation of the higher ideals that an earlier age once claimed for it. Central to that process must be a willingness to grapple with fundamental questions about music, questions that are asked neither by the classical musical establishment nor the popular culture in which classical music must now contend to be heard. What makes this music so important? How does it have any claim over the vast majority of people who aren't interested in it? Why does it privilege the claims of "great works" over those of ordinary people? The remaining chapters form one attempt to answer such questions.

CHAPTER 2. USES AND ABUSES

Music does things for us and to us. We use it in different ways to mediate our experiences of the world and ourselves. Its capacity to shape those experiences and to define our self-awareness is the subject of myth and legend and a fact of everyday life. That such symbolic mediations can have a power and a reality greater than the everyday is an important characteristic of our symbol-dominated culture. My argument is based on the idea that we value music for what it does for us and that our musical choices reflect these values. Individually, we often make different musical choices in different social contexts, because we expect music to fulfill a range of functions for us in those contexts. Our judgment about the same piece of music can change completely depending on its context.

A piece of avant-garde music, for example, heard on the radio, might be dismissed as "rubbish" by the same person who finds it "good" (i.e., extremely effective) as the score to a horror film. By the same token, I might find the music to a film thrilling while I watch the film but rather dull presented as autonomous music in a concert hall. I expect music to fulfill quite different functions in the two contexts. We do this all the time. We have little difficulty in identifying music that is "good for" a funeral as opposed to a children's party, background music for a shopping center as opposed to music for a military parade, and so on. Furthermore, we recognize that a certain music is "good" at fulfilling certain functions even if we would not judge the music as "good in itself" if it were removed from that function. In other words, we can appreciate and even enjoy music in certain social contexts but might not use that music privately, in our own domestic space. This is important because it highlights that our musical judgments are much more astute and broad-minded once we are aware of social function. What we might think of as the functionless activity of private listening also constitutes a function of music, but one that we consider so "natural" and ubiquitous that we think its standard could be applied universally.

This is the first and most common barrier to thinking about music and considering the partiality of our judgments. Most everyday uses of music function as background to some other activity. Those who design radio programs understand this very well and select different kinds of music for different times of day. Music aimed at commuters on their way home, for example, is likely to be more mellow and relaxing than the upbeat and energetic music played to the same commuters in the morning. Music played in shopping malls is most effective when it encourages people to take their time and feel at ease and when it suggests an air of classic, rich living. All this is obvious enough. But what about those times when people actively choose a certain kind of music, when listening is a more deliberate activity? Here again, we largely make choices according to function. What we want the music to "do" determines our choice. Most people have a sense of what music they would choose to make them feel a certain way. Or, more accurately, people choose certain musics at certain times knowing that they produce certain complex and indefinable effects. So we "feel like" some Billie Holiday now, or some Bach, or some Jimi Hendrix.

In essence, these choices are not so different from the ones we make, or that are made for us, about the background music that surrounds us at home or when we are out shopping. In both cases the music is chosen either to complement and reinforce our existing mood or to help change it. Much background music, particularly music on the radio, is used primarily to fill time. That we use music so often to stave off boredom, to fill temporal space that would otherwise seem empty, suggests that silence makes us anxious, that our culture suffers from a collective *horror vacui*. We often use music to "help time pass"—as if, without music, time would grind to a terrifying halt. This filling of time and manipulation of mood accounts for the majority of music-use in the developed world. It applies to a diverse range of musics and listeners and certainly applies as much to the use of classical music as it does to various popular musics. This function is so overwhelming that many people would find it hard to conceive of any other. It becomes normative in the sense that it comes to define what music is.

This normative definition of what music is *for* obscures the difference between musical judgments made by quite different criteria. What passes for debate under deceptive titles like "Is Mozart better than Madonna?" is usually nonsense because it presumes that these very different kinds of music serve the same function. That they are oriented around different functions is underlined by the fact that they are made differently. Their specific musical differences lend themselves to different functions. Music is thus no more a completely subjective matter than any other symbolic form. While different people, at different times, inevitably respond differently to the same piece of music, this difference is not infinitely variable. The idea of art presumes that the object is prior to the act of reception. People may leave the cinema with a variety of emotional experiences, but *Schindler's List* is not a comedy, is not set in the future, and is not about a giant ape called Kong. It does something different than a Disney cartoon.

And so it is with Mozart and Madonna. They are functionally equivalent only if one treats them in the most general way: they are both "music" just as *Schindler's List* and *Toy Story* are both films. But just as these two films do different things because they are made differently, so do Mozart and Madonna, and for the same reason. Approaches that focus only on reception and social use often ignore this basic fact, taking the functional equivalence of the recorded object as indicative of a wider equivalence. Only in specifically musical terms do their differences become apparent: they are made of different musical materials that are organized in different ways. Neither is understood by the criteria of the other: Mozart is outdated and makes for poor dance music, and Madonna's music lacks the sophistication of phrasing and form found in Mozart.

Nothing illustrates this situation better than the case of modernist or avant-garde music, which resolutely refuses to satisfy the function of confirming or creating "mood." Its frequent and abrupt changes make it very bad mood music and its cultivated unfamiliarity precludes it from acting as background to other activities. Judged by the prevailing popular criteria of good music (i.e., successful at reinforcing or creating a certain mood), most avant-garde music fails completely. In this it is not alone, however. As shopping-mall and restaurant compilations prove by what they exclude, a good deal of classical music is judged to be bad mood music, too. The best music for this purpose tends toward what baroque theory called a "unity of affect"—in other words, music that tends to create one mood or emotion by doing one main thing. Movements of baroque concertos exemplify this, as do most pop ballads—hence their popularity in these compilations. Certain pieces of classical and romantic music have this quality (and so recur again and again on CD compilations of classical music with titles like *Classic Moods* or *Classic Relaxation*), but a great many do not. The first movement of Beethoven's *Moonlight Sonata* works well in this context, but the final movement of the same sonata does not. By the same token, the Adagietto of Mahler's Fifth Symphony is popular in a way that the Scherzo from the same symphony is not—and so on.

The difference between the two is not hard to summarize. In a word, what remains unpopular about classical music is its *discursive* aspect. The claim of classical music is that, in order to make musical sense, it requires concentrated attention from start to finish. In some ways it is comparable to a rather involved novel or film; if you skip a few chapters or leave the room for a while, you may well lose the plot or narrative thread. One can put a novel down (literally) and take it up again without losing the narrative sense. Until the availability of sound and video recording in the home, this was not true of music or film. But most of us now possess the technical freedom to do just this. I can pause Beethoven halfway through a symphony, answer the telephone, and return where I left off. In some ways this is like putting the book down and beginning again in the same place; but in other ways, it is like answering the phone in the middle of making love and trying to begin again from where you left off.

In fact, the technological capacity of the medium (book, CD, video) to be placed on hold is of less significance here than the nature of the discourse it records. You could miss several minutes from scenes in most action movies without losing the plot. Equally, most dance music does not depend on making sequential links between its parts; it often does the same thing all the way through or alternates different elements without any cumulative, dramatic, or logical denouement. This music defines a certain mood, atmosphere, or musical space rather than producing any kind of narrative or discourse. Certain pieces of classical music may lend themselves to this approach, but, critically, many do not. Virtually all classical music, however one decides to listen to it, is structured on basically discursive lines. Fundamentally, this has to do with its use of harmony and the kind of musical forms to which that harmonic use gives rise, forms that in their long-range linearity and development are analogous to literary narrative. The nineteenth-century sonata or symphony is, in many ways, comparable to the nineteenth-century novel, though usually more concise. The musical "plot" becomes hard to follow if details are missed. While grand public forms allow for some redundancy, in chamber music and miniature forms the degree of concision is often exaggerated, requiring a particularly high degree of concentration if the music is not to sound like an involved but meaningless conversation.

This characteristic is doubtless the single most important factor in making large parts of the classical repertoire apparently inaccessible to a wider audience. The music developed in tandem with an aesthetic and social context that presented it as the object of focused or even rapt attention. It would be a mistake to think that this was ever the norm throughout society: it is a mode of listening almost exclusively associated with classical music, based on the ideal mode of listening to liturgical music and, indeed, the liturgy itself. The idea of a special space for music and a special mode of listening has come under frequent criticism recently and is often seen as an outdated nineteenth-century concept. But we understand that films are best viewed on large screens in darkened rooms (cinemas) and that to get the most out of them we need a modicum of silence and a certain degree of attention, just as most contemporary dance music is more effective if played at loud volume with all the visual effects associated with clubs and live concerts. It's not that films and music can't be heard outside of these venues, but we nevertheless understand that to gain maximum benefit we must submit to the demands of the object itself.

I am not arguing for the absolute rightness of a certain approach to classical music or to value one kind of listening over another. Rather, I am suggesting that discursive music is unlikely to fulfill its distinctive functions if approached undiscursively; moreover, it is unlikely to be very meaningful at all if approached as background music. Predominant uses of music in daily life tend to reinforce a distracted mode of listening that favors certain kinds of music, many of which are deliberately designed for it, but that fails to make sense of much classical music. One consequence of this is worrisome: in time, the possibility of a different approach to music becomes unthinkable to large numbers of people. One becomes deaf to the distinctive claims of a music that are heard only in relation to a different kind of listening. This has serious consequences. Classical music, inasmuch as it is to survive commercially in this environment, is forced into serving functions derived from entertainment music. Some classical music does this successfully; other classical music does not.

The idea of doing nothing else besides listening to music, for any sustained period of time, is foreign to many people. While virtually all of us use music, it is probably quite rare for people to focus exclusively on the music itself for long periods. It is far more common for our attention to drift in and out of focus as we think about or attend to other things. Many people's attention is the least diverted when music plays an ancillary role, as with dance music and film or TV music. A simplistic division has tended to equate classical music with concentrated, active listening and popular music with distracted, passive listening. This is, at best, outdated. It draws on a particular historical social use of these musics that meant classical music was almost always presented in a formal concert situation and popular music was often a background to other things. One of the effects of recording technology and its accessibility has been the leveling of differences between classical and popular music in this respect. Both can be experienced live, but both are more likely to be experienced through recording technology, a fact that allows them both to serve equivalent domestic functions, to be the object of more or less distracted listening.

Historically, much classical music was the object of distracted listening anyway. The opera house was, for most of its history, more like a combination of clubhouse and restaurant than the quasi sacred temple it has become. The high seriousness and aesthetic idealism that usually characterize today's opera house and concert hall developed in the nineteenth century amid and against a use of the same music that was far less formal. Retrospectively, the new attitude was associated with Beethoven, who was credited with (or blamed for) demanding this high seriousness, for writing music that was increasingly beyond the technical abilities of the amateur and demanded the concentration of rows of passive listeners before a virtuosic performer who stood in for the virtuosic genius of the composer.

But this caricature—true in part—is hardly applicable to a composer like Bach, whose music, while composed as functional music for the community in which he lived, nevertheless exhibits intricacies of form virtually unparalleled in Western music. Even the most educated listener is unlikely to follow the elaboration of parts in a six-part fugue or spot the perfection of his inverted and retrograde canons. Perhaps his music is like the ornate roof of Milan Cathedral, intended for the pleasure of God alone, and certainly we can take satisfaction from his music even if we understand nothing of these formal complexities. But how do we understand such extraordinary elaboration in a secular world? Today it may well be less meaningful to us that Bach, like Beethoven, Stravinsky, or Messiaen, contented himself that all this was ultimately "to the glory of God." But even in the most secular terms, such works are an invitation to participate in a formal complexity and sense of elaboration that exceeds that of our everyday lives. Sometimes entering a cathedral or coming across a particular landscape offers something similar: the invitation to participate in a larger reality, something that exceeds our own immediate experience and thought.

Such formal elaboration is at odds with many of the ways classical music is used today. It is at odds with its use in restaurants, shopping malls, and elevators, on telephone answering machines, and in a host of other contexts that formally contradict the demands of its own musical logic— demands that it be heard in its entirety and detail. Because the consequence of these uses and the technologies that make them possible is that not only does our attention to the music tend to be distracted, but the music can be cut off at any moment. When our car journey ends and we turn off the engine, the music stops. The telephone answering machine may give us thirty seconds of Mozart, only to interrupt it when our call is put through. Such uses (and they are built into the CD, the remote control, and the whole notion of a personal hi-fi) tend to work against one of the most basic traditional assumptions of classical music—the primacy of its temporal form.

One understands that a novel makes best sense when read in its entirety and that if you leave a play after the first act, it will probably be less satisfying than seeing the whole thing. Most people stay to the end of the film. Classical music is designed in a similar way; its distinctive sense and meaning are gleaned by hearing a piece in its entirety. Its formal consistency is part of the music's meaning. Hear only a chunk of it and this consistency is lost. Classical music can be and often is used in other ways, but then the music is valued not for itself but as a sign for something else. Individually and collectively, we exercise our right to use music in this way. We may similarly exercise our right to use Shakespeare's collected works as a doorstop or a Rodin bust as a paperweight, but in each case the object's design suggests its potential for more fruitful employment.

USE AND FUNCTION

It is a central idea of aesthetics that art has no immediate function. Since Kant, writing at the end of the eighteenth century, art's value has been linked to its autonomy, its separation from the functional demands of everyday life. Popular culture, on the other hand, is bound up with everyday uses that high art seems to shun in preference for the "functionless" activity of aesthetic contemplation. Popular culture not only deals with materials from daily life far more directly; its use is also far more directly tied into everyday life. High culture is generally more removed from the everyday and, where it makes reference to daily life, often does so only obliquely and allusively. In the case of music, especially instrumental music, overt reference to the everyday is almost entirely lacking. I think this division is misleading and that it is possible to talk about all types of music in terms of use and function. Indeed, we must do so, because the functions that different types of music imply vary widely. This seems to contradict a key stage in traditional aesthetics that insist on a "disinterested" approach to the artwork, but it is only an apparent contradiction. Artworks *are* valued for what they do but not for any *immediate* function. Art is far from "useless," even though its distinctive value is realized only when it serves no *immediate* function, when the viewer or listener gives up any immediate self-centered demands on the work and, instead, gives him- or herself up to the work. The famous "disinterestedness" demanded by Kant is thus a relative term.

There is, however, an important distinction between the everyday uses to which music is put and the underlying and often unconscious functions it may also fulfill. Music usually involves us in more than we are aware. We choose a certain music because we find it good to dance to or because we like the emotional drama of grand opera, but our participation also often helps define us both to ourselves and to other members of our social group. We may choose a single style or deliberately cross boundaries between different musical types. This is probably more common today than it used to be, in part because the boundaries between social identities have become more fluid. We use music as a medium for self-articulation, as a way of defining ourselves, and we invest in it in profoundly personal ways. The music we identify with often becomes inseparable from our self-identity, such that we experience certain music as a statement of ourselves. For this reason, we often identify in an intensely personal manner with certain performers or composers.

To experience music as a statement of ourselves and an expression of our feelings somehow more complete than we might have been able to articulate alone invests music with great weight and responsibility. Above all, we invest it with a quality of "truth" or "authenticity" that hinges on that of the composer or performer who delivers it: they speak truthfully for us, we believe, because they speak truthfully from themselves. Authenticity of self-expression has thus become a touchstone of musical quality and value. Conversely, music is most often dismissed when it is presumed to be lacking authenticity. It is considered inauthentic for different reasons: it may be deemed superficial, clichéd, formulaic, conventional, derivative, and cheap, but also academic, intellectual, mathematical, abstract, and esoteric. Music, according to this dominant position, should be the true expression of true feeling. Its truth is guaranteed not so much by the music's technical attributes as by the authenticity of the composer or performer. If it is truly personal, it will be original. And in this originality of the artist's personal voice, we believe we recognize our own unique individuality. Because music is a collective language, we recognize ourselves as unique individuals within a community of individuals.

At each stage the essential idea is self-expression; the composer writes and the performer plays in order to express themselves through the music, and listeners, too, find something of themselves expressed in the music. The problem with this model is that it is inferred from the listener back to the composer. *Because* listeners feel deeply moved and believe that the music in some way speaks for them, they infer the sincerity and intensity of self-expression on behalf of the performer and composer. This is often simply not the case, as every musician knows. One can bring audiences to tears with a string of sentimental clichés, none of which are delivered with sincerity by the performer, who no longer believes in them. Musicians often take on the role of characters that, as in the theater or on the screen, bear little resemblance to their own personality. Music does not always repay the trust that is invested in it, and the faith that what one finds "good" is thereby "authentic" music may well be misplaced. This will cause consternation for those who believe that the intensity of their own emotional response is sufficient proof of the music's quality and therefore authenticity, but this is no more true of music than it is of other symbolic languages. When the emotional responses aroused by political orators have been taken as a measure of their truth, social disaster has usually ensued.

The concept of authenticity presumes the possibility of "pseudo-authenticity," a posturing that makes use of all the signs of sincere self-expression but that is merely learned and conventionalized. To nonmusicians the art of music remains something of a mystery, verging on the magical. But to trained musicians it soon becomes apparent that, like any symbolic language, music has its familiar figures of speech, its rhetorical devices and, indeed, its clichés. Having genuine intentions or big emotions is no guarantee of success in music that, like all art, involves a skill in making things that is not necessarily given simply because one has strong feelings.

The nineteenth-century writer Eduard Hanslick suggested that to judge music solely by the emotions it aroused was like trying to judge a wine while getting drunk. Maintaining a critical distance means remaining skeptical that because musical works evoke an intense emotional response, they therefore exhibit "authentic expression." The whole idea of music as expression, let alone self-expression, is deeply problematic. Contemporary thought tends to favor the idea that music *constructs* rather than *expresses* a self, and that it offers subjective "positions" by which composers and listeners alike orient themselves, as opposed to theories of expression centered on an essentialist notion of some central or static self.

Whichever approach one takes, there is a distinction to be made between the outward social use of music and its inner construction. Music not only signifies subject positions outwardly, placing its adherents culturally and socially; it also does so inwardly. And these two modes of signifying are not necessarily in unison with each other. Music that outwardly signifies fashionable modernity may be utterly conventional internally. Music that outwardly signifies a tolerant, liberal lifestyle may inwardly exhibit repressive tendencies. If this sounds strange, perhaps that is because the *inward* signification of music is so neglected today that the whole question of musical meaning is addressed almost entirely in terms of its outward signification.

Like any other musical style, classical music acts as a sign for cultural and subjective positions. But it is misunderstood by a form of cultural studies that reads its meaning entirely in these terms rather than in tension with its richly elaborated inward meanings. From the perspective of cultural analysis alone, classical music is clearly associated with a range of positions capable of both a positive and negative inflection. It comes to stand as a cultural sign whose function has more to do with the epithet "classical" than the music itself. It can thus stand for a broad range of interrelated signifieds: wealth, class, exclusive quality, craftsmanship, luxury, precision, formality, education, social responsibility and power, tradition, and so on.

Outwardly, music can and frequently does function as a signpost in this way. But this approach remains inadequate as a tool for fully understanding music. The outward signifying of music is certainly an important aspect of music's social use, but it remains the most basic level of musical significance. What signifies here is not the music itself, in all its elaborate detail, but merely its outward surface or style. Where this perspective dominates, music shrinks to the status of an empty sign. Observations that may well be important sociological facts become untrue as statements about music if the account stops at this point, as if the thing itself—music—had no existence or substantiality of its own, as if this richly structured and historically eloquent thing were no more internally significant than a road sign or a bank note. Understanding music only as a sign for other things ultimately reflects the logic of the marketplace and a consciousness that cannot conceive of something in and for itself but only as infinitely exchangeable for other things.

There is a place for indexing and cataloging current social uses of music. But thinking about music should not be equivalent to its social use. It should consider the difference between how the musical object is used and what it might be aside from that use. That, after all, is the difference between cataloging and thinking. It is instructive to demonstrate how modern media (such as advertising) tend to reduce music to a functional equivalence (i.e., a sign system for other things, such as social attributes or social position). But thinking about music should not simply reproduce this social fact; it should reflect on the disjunction between the *apparent* equivalence implied by such uses and the qualitative material differences exhibited by the musics themselves.

CLASSICAL MUSIC AS POPULAR CULTURE

Music in popular culture often functions as part of a wider system of fashion. This has several important consequences for how music is considered and the functions it is expected to fulfill. Chief among these is the fact that music becomes a vehicle for expressing a wider cultural position or style. The question of musical style is here analogous to clothing style: what matters most is the position certain things signify and the context in which they are used, rather than their intrinsic qualities. Articulating one's own sense of self-identity and relation to larger social groups through music, just as with clothes, hinges on adopting certain cultural positions at certain times, while remaining responsive to how the sign system of which they are a part is constantly shifting. Last year's music is dropped, like last year's clothes, not because it is literally "worn out" but because it no longer functions as the sign of a *current* position.

In this context, music, like fashion, is cultural currency in a double sense: it functions as a sign of value but only by "being current." While we may have a certain nostalgic affection for the music we shed in earlier parts of our lives, it apparently falls behind us as inevitably as time itself. We laugh at the clothes we wore ten years ago and the ways we decorated our homes, the cars we considered stylish. Of course, classical music may seem little affected by this pattern of contemporary fashion. Its classical status rests on a claim to be outside this process and so far removed from the contemporary that it possesses a certain timeless quality—precisely the intention of the epithet "classical" applied to clothes and furniture as much as to music. But it *is* affected because thinking about music as an element of fashion is at odds with thinking about music-as-art. And this thinking is so dominant and ubiquitous that the aesthetic claims on which the distinctive value of classical music depends are rarely heard or understood today. They depend on categories of thinking about music that are simply not part of the dominant way of thinking about music as fashion.

Most important, the objective judgments about music itself from which positions in classical music are derived have little meaning in a popular context. Here, judgments about music are made and frequently discussed, but they are understood to be linked to specific groups and situations, beyond which they often have little application. Not only are judgments locally determined (rather than absolute), but expression of musical opinions becomes an important part of defining a certain cultural space or locality. Musical tastes and our expressions of them are important elements of social interaction; they place us, and (like sport and fashion) they bind us together in subtle ways. And the more plural contemporary culture becomes, the greater the social need to define ourselves by making cultural judgments and articulating allegiances. In this process, the truth of judgments, in an absolute sense, is irrelevant. What matters is the activity of agreement and dispute, aligning oneself with certain positions and groups and differentiating oneself from others. Where music functions in this way, to define social space or membership in a certain group, it is analogous to the way a corporate logo or a national flag might function. What matters has less to do with the object's aesthetic quality and more to do with the complex signaling of identification and difference that the sign represents and accomplishes. Signs such as national flags, team colors, and anthems elicit strong feelings. Singing the national anthem on the football field before an international game may stir deep emotion, while hardly being emotive or expressive from a purely musical point of view.

Today, identification with a certain kind of music is often inseparable from identification with a singer or group and thus with a larger network of signs that collectively define a wider cultural position. In contemporary commercial music this cultural position is fundamentally allied to a statement of fashion position: a definition of how one is placed within contemporary fashion. The music as such is one part of an integrated web of signs that reflect visual image and style as much as music. To identify with the music of x or y is almost always to identify, to some degree at least, with their cultural position, attitude, style, viewpoint, sexuality, politics, and so on. This compulsion to identify is not restricted to contemporary culture; there used to be a considerable market for miniature busts of the great composers, which were lined up on the mantelpiece like a collection of household gods, and opera singers have habitually attracted fans on the same scale as pop idols. In an age when classical musicians, and indeed the classical legacy itself, is often marketed in ways derived from commercial music, it is necessary to underline the distinction between music that merely forms part of a complex package of cultural signifiers and a quite different approach that regards a piece of music as possessing an objective identity of its own.

Equally important here is that contemporary commercial music is, above all, the music of youth. Young people spend more time and money on music than any other sector of society, and since our cultural diet is primarily market-led, it follows that our dominant musical culture is that of youth. But the commercial value and cultural ubiquity of youth music should not be confused with questions of musical value *beyond* the social milieu for which it is primarily significant. In other words, youth music *seems* much more important than it is. This music is used, like other areas of fashion, as part of teenage rites of passage that include formulating individual identities in relation to collective groups, articulating independence from a parental generation, and coping with excess libidinal energy in the absence of other obvious outlets for it. Youth not only literally carve out their own cultural space by playing their music (indoors and out); they have also done so figuratively in terms of cultural airtime. Later in life, the music may be retained as a nostalgic memento of those years (as a particularly vivid form of memory), but otherwise its importance generally declines as one moves into adult life. So a large part of the discussion of popular music properly belongs to the sociology or anthropology of youth rather than to a strictly musical inquiry.

The overwhelming presence of this music, a product of the economic power of youth, guarantees its popularity by the circular process of commercial saturation. More than that, it appears to take on a cultural importance out of all proportion to the age group whose advocacy has placed it there. What remains hard to understand is why adult culture should also be shaped to such a degree by what is, after all, youth culture. But the distinction I am making is of course not clearly defined in contemporary culture. Our collective fascination with the imagery of youth and youthfulness effectively dissolves any boundaries between the cultural diets of children, adolescents, and adults. Seven-year-old children and thirty-seven-year-old adults are equally fascinated, it seems, by a musical culture defined almost exclusively by the images of singers between the ages of seventeen and twenty-seven.

Not only is classical music not oriented so exclusively; quite the opposite is usually the case. Most composers have to pass through a long period of unofficial apprenticeship before calling a work their "Opus 1," and even child prodigies are generally more celebrated for their late works than their early ones. Composers' late works, often written in old age, have a special quality, a depth and sophistication that exceeds the masterpieces of their earlier periods; one thinks of late Haydn, Beethoven, Verdi, Wagner, and Tippett. Leos Janáček wrote his most celebrated works in his sixties and seventies, and these works remain distinctive for their radical and personal style, as well as for their sheer energy and passion. Such examples show that classical music makes a quite different proposition: it is no less concerned with individuality, radical difference, and expansive energy, but it does not restrict these qualities to the image of a merely physical youthfulness.

Recent marketing of classical music shows conspicuous signs of drawing on the style, imagery, and strategies of marketing popular music. But however photogenic certain performers may be, classical music will never serve as a cultural image of youthfulness in the same way. It is not part of a wider fashion function, and the importance of one piece over another has nothing to do with where it is placed in terms of fashion (either today's fashion or that of the time in which it is written). Fashions come and go in classical music, too, albeit on a larger time scale (witness the sudden popularity of Mahler in the 1960s), but in general a classical musician is likely to value music from a wide range of styles, at least from Mozart to Puccini, if not from Josquin to Birtwistle.

Because classical music fits neither the demands of musical fashion nor the construction of an imagery of youth, it falls by the wayside in a contemporary musical culture dominated by those ideals. In some ways this is ironic. The idea of transgression, of breaking rules, for example, is every bit as important to classical music as it is to popular music, but one is essentially an inward, musical matter while the other is an outward, performative display. An important adolescent rite of passage, for which music often serves as a vehicle, hinges on the ritualized transgressive acts by which a parental culture is symbolically rejected. Inwardly, the musical materials and their deployment in such acts are often largely conventional. Classical music, at least before the twentieth century, rarely exhibits outwardly transgressive moments, but inwardly, within the musical discourse itself, it is frequently predicated on the idea of exceeding its own formal boundaries, of a radical reformulation of its materials and a transgression of the boundaries of the familiar.

It is bemusing that classical music is so often characterized as conventional, conservative, and formulaic, and yet the moment it becomes audibly not so—in Schoenberg or Stravinsky—it is dismissed for being incomprehensible. But the elements modernism brings to the surface of music are also a feature of earlier classical music. The disjunctions, reformulations, and transgressions of boundaries, so central to Beethoven's music, are missed only by an approach to the music that stops at the outward signs of classicism. Again, if it seems odd to claim that Beethoven may be more transgressive than punk or heavy metal, this, too, reflects a tendency to read musical meaning only on the outer surface of musical practice rather than in its inner detail. The transgressions of popular culture seem more weighty than those of classical music because they are more immediate and more concrete, but they are also more ephemeral. The radical proposition of Schoenberg's music has hardly ameliorated since he wrote it, nearly a century ago. Similarly, the transgressions of a Schoenberg or a Picasso are not the gestures of adolescence, left behind for a more conventional adult life. Their transgressions are lifelong because they are more than simple refusals. Such art is concerned with the permanent reformulation of aesthetic elements—not merely a rejection of something, but the projection of an alternative vision.

Classical music, like art more generally, cannot be understood in the terms of popular culture. It is concerned with details of its musical language and inner musical form to a degree that popular music is not. Its value has little to do with fashion or the particular social rituals of any one stage of life. My point is not to oppose the two musics or to play one off against the other but to insist that classical music-as-art will never be understood in terms of the criteria applied to popular music. This should make us question the criteria's validity and the functions derived from popular music as universal yardsticks of musical value.

The distinctive historical claims of music-as-art are no longer heard when the term "art" becomes indistinguishable from terms like "culture," "entertainment," and "leisure." Art becomes one of an interchangeable list of activities or pastimes people engage in when they are not at work. Most people are aware of a difference between what public institutions (galleries, concert halls, and theaters) define as art and a more colloquial use of the term to refer to almost anything that demonstrates great skill or is considered attractive. But while we may not usually reflect on why that division exists, we often challenge others' use of the term and are defensive if our own use of it is questioned. Because "art" has come to refer to something highly valued, the term is inevitably contested. Even people who don't care much about art can argue passionately that something is or isn't art. The term still functions as an accolade; to call something "art" is to invest it with all the value that has accrued around such objects in the past. It is to claim that the object is quite different from other human artifacts and to give it an aura usually reserved for sacred objects in religious cultures.

To claim some music as art is to imply that other music is not art, or at least that some music is *more* like art, or *better* art than other music. Art is frequently contrasted with entertainment, an opposition that immediately invokes a series of binary divisions (e.g., high and low, serious and light, intellectual and sensual) that seem like so many aesthetic versions of opposing class positions. Indeed, for some, the difference between art and entertainment has no aesthetic meaning, only a sociological one, being a difference that attempts to mask a social divide even as it reproduces it. But such divisions are misleading about art that was traditionally not wholly separate from the idea of entertainment.

Art and entertainment are perhaps better understood as social functions than as categories that divide cultural products as if they were sheep and goats. Classical music, I have argued, is made as art but frequently serves as entertainment. Even when it serves as art, it doesn't necessarily stop serving as entertainment. But it also exhibits qualities that are neither acknowledged nor accounted for by the category of entertainment, qualities that can be understood only from the expectations of a different function—that of art. These qualities are objective (in that they are qualities of the art object) and are separable from the responses they arouse in different listeners. But this is not to say that any particular quality is definitive of art, as opposed to entertainment, because the qualities that allow a work to function as art are historical rather than factual in a scientific sense.

The insistence on a division between art and entertainment arose as art opposed the idea of entertainment as its sole function. Prior to modernism, entertainment was a central category of artworks, albeit one that could not of its own adequately account for art. Modernism may be partly understood as a rebellion against the tendency to lose sight of the tension signaled by the theoretical difference between art and entertainment, a refusal to accept that art could be defined according to the criteria of entertainment. Modern music—perhaps even more than its visual counterpart—stridently denies the listener the chance to treat it merely as entertainment. It cannot be understood except on terms that art demands and that entertainment does not and, in doing so, it frustrates and annoys those whose definition of music rests on principles derived from entertainment.

In this way, the modern music crisis is the clearest sign of the legitimation crisis facing classical music as a whole, but the crisis is masked where that music has been absorbed into an entertainment culture. In these cases, classical music has to function according to the criteria of an entertainment culture, criteria that marginalize and obscure its definitive claim to other functions. Music-as-art differs from music-as-entertainment in one important way: it places greater emphasis on musical form than on the sensual qualities of musical sounds for their own sake. Of course, the sounds are often quite similar: plenty of musical styles employ a standard symphony orchestra, for example. But music-as-art is distinguished by its particular focus on the patterning of those sounds, their complex elaboration, and the sequence of the musical process as the work unfolds. It does not so much shun the qualities of musical sounds themselves; rather, it uses them as a vehicle for musical thought, as opposed to isolated moments of physical pleasure. But music-as-art is inadequately described by this dualistic opposition of sensuous materials on the one hand and abstract thought on the other, and neither the word "intellectual" nor the word "spiritual" captures its essential activity: the projection of that definitively human awareness of being more than the sum of one's material parts.

This activity has made music-as-art a central medium in the development of Western thought and sensibility, as well as a powerful force in shaping modern ideas of subjectivity, freedom, and the relation of the individual to the world. Its discursive aspect—its concern with the real world but in aesthetic form—lies behind its apparently introverted concern with its own formal and material components. Once again, this is underlined by the way modern classical music believes that its authenticity is bound up with the historical logic of its language.

The introversion of classical music, its turning away from the everyday world, is antithetical to a popular aesthetic defined by a greater proximity to the everyday. Art, in contrast, is characterized by a fracture or disjunction between lived and aesthetic experience. Why should this be valuable? What is there to be gained by art's self-conscious concern with form and thereby its distance (or even refusal) of an apparently more "human" element? Art often deals with the everyday (most obviously painting and literature), but it does not simply reproduce it. It takes up the everyday in order to rework it, to reshape and reformulate, and thus to offer back a refracted version. In the distance between the real everyday and its aesthetic reworking lies art's capacity for critique and utopian suggestion. Art's capacity for escapist illusion is derived, of course, in exactly the same way.

But sometimes art is not obviously concerned with the everyday. It is concerned with the extraordinary, the outer limits of our experience, and often an interior experience at that. This, again, has two contradictory aspects: it is the source of art's unique value as a means of articulating areas of experience beyond everyday linguistic discourse, and at the same time it is a means of becoming fantasy, more or less unrelated to the concerns of the everyday. Art's apparent refusal of the everyday is not a refusal of the "human" as such: it is a refusal of the idea that the sum of what it is to be human is found in the everyday. By the same token, popular culture's refusal of art comes close to an affirmation of the everyday as a closed universe, a confirmation of things as they are, an ideological capitulation to immediacy. A rejection of art's difference from the everyday is thus a rejection of a central claim of an enlightened humanism: that the condition of our lives and our being is held in tension with a sense of a greater condition and a greater being. Art speaks to a fundamental human longing to realize ourselves as something greater than we are, a longing that forms both the core and the origin of genuine artworks. A theory of art has to wrestle with the fact that, in a materialist society, this longing appears in distorted form at the heart of class distinctions, but it is a distortion that theory should expose, not reproduce.

Art's claim to humanity is thus found precisely in its difference from the everyday. Its reworking of material elements of human life requires a delicate balance, one that has changed in different historical moments. Music is too often dismissed as abstract, and classical instrumental music most obviously so. And yet classical music at its inception was clearly related to the everyday, both in terms of its vernacular musical materials and the social space it inhabited. Mozart's operas, with their democratic put-down of bumbling aristocrats, were enjoyed equally by a popular audience and the aristocracy they parodied, and Haydn's quartets were not infrequently played in pubs. The humanity of classical music, as projected by a Haydn string quartet or a Mozart opera, lies in its projection of an aristocracy of the spirit that is the democratic birthright of all. It falls to the anti-Enlightenment elements within Enlightenment itself to reduce this metaphysical aspiration to the one-dimensional materialism of class divisions.

Classical music's claims exceed the social functions to which it has been too often reduced. But they are realized only when the music is treated not as a sign for something else (social status, wealth, education) but as the sole object of one's interest. The capacity of classical music—what it might do for us—is paradoxically realized only by a concentration on the musical object rather than on ourselves. All the talk of self-expression and identity, of social signs and positions, obscures a definitive moment on which art depends: that of *encounter*. Ascribing to music the capacity for self-expression is often a sleight-of-hand for the listener's self-projection. But self-projection runs counter to art's definitive value, the encounter in the artwork of something other than oneself, the experience of something beyond one's experience and habitual ordering of the world. This "something" often challenges us to the core—an experience that can be had from the most "familiar" piece of Mozart just as much as from the unfamiliar territory of the avant-garde. What this encounter might involve and why it should exercise such power over us is the subject of the following chapters.

CHAPTER 3. MUSIC AS ART

To talk of art implies the priority of an object over our perception. How people habitually perceive and interpret things is an important question, but it is not ultimately related to the question of art's *potential*. If perception is not shaped by the object, then one is no longer talking about art at all. And if it seems strange that one should accord primacy to something that is meant to be a tool of one's pleasure, perhaps that is because the concept of art as something distinct has been all but lost in contemporary culture. The objective differences between a Brahms symphony and elevator music are neither arbitrary nor irrelevant. Whatever people's responses to them may be, these texts make different objective demands of the listener and different musical statements. The structural and linguistic differences between musical objects invite different responses from their listeners, who remain free at all times, of course, to project whatever feelings they like upon the work.

But to most people music is not an object at all; it is a mood, an ambience, an environment, and is mostly used to that end. This contrasts strongly with the way music is regarded by professional musicians such as composers, performers and musicologists. The professional is necessarily concerned with how a musical work is made—with notes, chords, instrumentation, structure, and form, rather than sound alone or the pleasure of musical experience. But the nonmusician needs to be concerned with these aspects no more than the fan of Grand Prix racing needs to understand car mechanics or the gourmet needs to understand food science. Neither the purely analytical nor the purely appetitive is wholly adequate as an approach to art, yet both derive from the same central paradox of the artwork: that it is a sensuous object and, at the same time, projects a patterning or form that is more than the sum of its sensuous parts.

Art is a complex thing in the same way that we are complex things. It has its being as a physical thing or event, but it is vivified by a thought or spirit that exceeds its existence as a mere object. As any painter, writer, or composer knows, artworks arise from the tension between their physical materials and the thought or spirit that shapes them from within. Though they require some outward, physical element, they cease to function as art when they are reduced to their objectlike, artifactual element. This definitive tension underlies art's varied social uses and explains how it came to be celebrated on the one hand as an expression of the highest spiritual achievements of humanity and, on the other, criticized as merely another precious object—a trapping of wealth, privilege, and social exclusion. Even in the heyday of classical music, there was always a gap between the philosophical claims for music and social practice. Its elevation to the highest intellectual and spiritual status by romantic writers around 1800 occurred just as its everyday social presence was ensured by its orientation around entertainment and distraction.

Significantly, at this time music also became an object in a new way. The expansion of commercial music printing for a growing market of amateur performers fundamentally altered the way music was conceived. Prior to that, the performances would have been thought of primarily as *music-making*—as a social practice attached to social gatherings such as religious services or communal celebrations. Since many musicians played or directed performances of their works, music had a very limited life beyond live performance. The widespread printing of sheet music and musical scores allowed music to become a tangible object like a book and thus a commodity whose use extended far beyond the sway of the composer. Significantly, musicians still refer to the printed page as "the music" just as much as to the sound that arises from its performance. This change had several consequences. It liberated the listener from the authority of the composer-performer. Sheet music made the work available anytime one cared to play it. Moreover, it could be used however one pleased. It could serve as the background to other things, such as playing cards or conversation, or as the vehicle for purely private reverie. And one could skip the difficult or less interesting passages and play the easier or more interesting moments again and again to oneself. As music became a thing, it became a private possession; the demands of the composer and of the musical work could be subordinated to the pleasures of the possessor.

It is no coincidence that this objectification of music was exactly contemporaneous with the rise of musical classicism. The publication of musical works shifted the balance away from music's generic role, as ancillary to other activities such as dancing or worship, toward the individual work for its own sake. This newfound autonomy of music, particularly instrumental music, went hand in hand with the idea of the classic work. The new musical consumer bought not just music "in general" but also this particular Beethoven piano sonata or that particular Schubert string quartet. Our view of individual works as unique and ultimately canonic texts is thus bound up with the status they derived through publication. This, in turn, goes hand in hand with a third definitive factor—the development of a new historical consciousness. Establishing the absolute canonic value of old masters, such as Palestrina, Bach, and Handel, legitimated the new self-consciousness of classical composers about the status of their own work.

The contradiction between the high aesthetic claims for classical music and its more down-to-earth social use is thus rooted in its origins. But changes effected by the commercial printing of music in the eighteenth century are nothing compared to those brought about by commercial sound recording in the twentieth century. The freedom of the amateur performer anticipates that of the twentieth-century listener but is different in several crucial respects. However inadequate a performer, the amateur musician always had to accord a certain primacy to the musical text, at least for the duration of his or her attempts to perform it. To be sure, you can start halfway through and give up before the end, or you can play a piece at half-speed peppered with wrong notes, but nevertheless your activity is shaped directly and often intensely by the demands of the musical text with which you are wrestling. You are bound to the text's unfolding progress just as you are bound to the instrument you are playing.

Sound recording changed all that. It may be that people listened to the earliest wax cylinders with a degree of concentration and attention identical to that expected in the concert hall. Some people may still listen to recorded music this way. But overwhelmingly, the ubiquity of recorded music and the variety of means for its reproduction has utterly changed the dominant social use of classical music. Above all, it separates the listener from the demands of music's temporal form. Sound recording literally turns music into an object, such as a CD, but more important, it allows music to function as a thing that one possesses rather than a structured temporal event to which one must give oneself up. Of course, books are possessed objects, too, but for all their cultural stockpiling, a book still demands that one hold the thing in front of one's face and be absorbed by it for the duration of one's reading. Without a certain level of engagement on the reader's behalf, reading a book simply doesn't work.

This is not felt to be true for music. While it is undoubtedly *possible* to listen to a CD with the same degree of engagement, sound recording allows music to happen in a way that makes no demand for us to enter into the temporal process of its unfolding. In fact, this seems almost inevitable. Contemporary uses of music as background to other things, functions that depend on the technology of the CD, the Walkman, and the car stereo, tend to flatten out the musical experience. As we cease to attend to the detailed sequence of musical events and the unfolding of their dynamic processes, the music takes on a certain uniformity of surface. The old metaphor of musical wallpaper is still useful, because it captures the degree to which music comes to function as ambient background, below the level of active consciousness and attention. It affects the atmosphere in important ways, like lighting or décor, but is essentially a static, atmospheric factor rather than a discursive process.

There is an obvious paradox here: the technologies of printing and recording that allow music its autonomy (its freedom from specific social rituals of everyday life) also allow music to be reabsorbed into everyday life. What distinguishes music as a discrete, autonomous object for aesthetic contemplation also collapses the distance between music and an ancillary, background function to everyday life. Sound recording, like all technologies, is a double-edged sword. It makes available musical possibilities that earlier ages could not have dreamed of: at a touch of a button, anywhere on the planet, I can access fantastic performances by leading international artists, dead and alive, of virtually any piece I might think of. But at the same time, a distinctive requirement of music-as-art, that one engage with its temporal unfolding within the discrete time of its performance, is displaced by the technologies of recorded sound. Live performance ensures that we accord a certain primacy to the musical work by forcing us to give in to its temporal processes. Recorded music reverses that equation by allowing us to subordinate the music to the demands of other activities: when our journey ends, the car stereo clicks off no matter where we are in the symphony.

It is no coincidence that these new technologies not only enable but ensure the dominance of the music that best complements them. Inevitably, the most popular musical forms today are not only miniatures, rarely more than a few minutes long, but are also effectively seamless in structure. They tend to do a single, essentially static thing that might repeat indefinitely or stop at almost any point. The fade-out thus remains a standard ending because seamless music, having no inward formal tension, can have only an arbitrary ending. Seamless music not only minimizes events that would break up its smooth surface; it also avoids any suggestion of a complex verticality, such as polyphony or harmonic complexity, that would detract from its deliberate depthlessness. Contemporary marketing has found ways to replicate this in compilations of short movements and excerpts that lend themselves to this mode of musical use, but this has little to do with classical music's capacity to function as art.

Classical music derives from an earlier technology, that of musical notation, whose apparently anachronistic persistence in composition is striking in the age of digital samplers and sequencers. But the opposition of paper and pencil on the one hand and computer and DAT recorders on the other points to a significant difference in the nature of musical objects. While notation is responsible for the idea of the score as a musical object, it also resists the idea of music being found in a particular object, forcing "the music" to hover somewhere between the performance and the score. The musical work is neither the score, the live performance, nor the recording; it exists somewhere between the idea of the work and its realization in performance. Notation also forces composers to work at a distance from the physicality of the sounds, so that composition becomes a more abstract, reflective activity. This contrasts with other kinds of musical invention that are governed by more direct responses to musical sounds, as in improvisation or work in an electronic studio.

The process of composition, then, is less immediate in the case of classical music—a fact well illustrated by the often protracted thought process traced out in composers' sketches. The classical composer works not so much with sounds themselves as with *ideas of sounds* and their patterning. Classical music is less immediate in other ways, too: crucially, it attaches less importance to the self-sufficiency of its sound world at any given moment and more to the unfolding process of the work. The music's content is not heard immediately but rather as the product of its unfolding through time. Its discursive, temporal narrative resists the kind of listening that tries to grasp it in a single brief moment, as a physical object. For its critics, of course, classical music often lacks the immediacy of more popular forms; for its supporters, its more mediate character gives it a different function and a different kind of value.

From the perspective of global musical cultures, detailed notation is both rare and slightly odd. But it is a defining factor in several classical traditions beyond Western classical music. And for better or worse, it has exerted a profound effect on the development of musical languages and forms within the traditions that depend on it. It is in no way simply a means of fixing music after the event, but rather a tool that allows for an extension and development of musical ideas that would not have been possible in an entirely oral culture. Moreover, the notation retains an independent life of its own. To imagine that the recording or the individual performance is the musical object in its entirety is to obscure the production process and to misunderstand the complex identity of a classical work. The score of a notated musical work implies that the music is more than a single performance or audition of it. In this way, a single act of

listening is similar to a single meeting with another person. For the duration of that meeting, I have the whole person before me; I engage with him
for a while, and then he is gone. Was the totality of that person exhausted
by my meeting with him? Was my response and the degree of pleasure
generated by that meeting an adequate measurement of the sum of that
person? So it is with art. The notated aspect of music, like the artifactual
quality of other artworks, functions as a symbol for the difference between
partial experience and knowledge of the whole. It is a representation of
our profound belief in the distance between appearance and essence. In
plain terms, our sense of being more than what others might make of us
in a single meeting, a self-awareness of our ungraspable wholeness and
uniqueness, forms the basis for our modern notion of individuality. And if
artworks function as a symbol of this, then our lack of respect for them,
the ease with which we appropriate them and define them by the quantity
and quality of pleasure they give us, is perhaps a sign of our lack of respect
for one another and for ourselves.

Classical music does not fare well in the context of contemporary technologies and the musical practices they enable. When music becomes a
static, ambient object, it loses its central category of form. Form in music
arises from temporal unfolding—from the differentiation of events and
materials, the patterning of their development and variation, contrast, interruption, and transcendence. Conversely, it is precisely the idea of form
that resists a contraction to a seamless, depthless surface that allows a temporal medium such as music to function as a kind of object. Form is therefore the vehicle of thought in music. Of course, music is a long way from
the abstraction of pure thought. Its sonorous immediacy, the physicality of
sound, strikes us with the force of a material object and elicits a reaction
that is primarily bodily. All music has this element. But music-as-art insists
on being more than that, on being the formal organization of this physical,
corporeal element through time, an aspect that is lost when the primacy of
music's temporal unfolding is denied.

It is denied today by habitual social practices in relation to music, the
recording technologies that make them possible, and the predominance of
music that fulfills those conditions by largely relinquishing the idea of temporal form. This is the real reason classical music fares badly today—not
because it is old but because it demands an engagement of the mind
through time (thought) that contemporary conceptions of music no
longer recognize. Classical music is at odds with contemporary culture
precisely because of its insistence on the tension between the bodily and
the intellectual, the material and the spiritual, the thinglike and its transcendence in thought. For it is striking that much of contemporary culture

appears to be in complete denial of this tension. I suggest, therefore, that classical music is today a form of cultural resistance: it opposes a process by which we reduce the world to opaque, depthless objects and, with it, ourselves. It becomes marginal precisely where it does not easily collude in this process.

It is a significant paradox of musical practice that, as music becomes a physical object as never before, its objective claims are ignored as never before. Contemporary reception, facilitated by the recorded musical object, masks that dependency by the illusions of modern technology. It implies that music simply exists, that it embraces us in a total, ambient universe, surrounding us at all times and thus dissolving the sense of any one direction or time. The fetish for surround-sound and total ambient control of music (turning acoustic space into a kind of amniotic space) aims to make the source of music somehow invisible and, denying its origin in technology, to make it "natural." This contrasts strongly with the apparently technologically redundant medium of live performance that perforce has to take place in a specific space and time. It has to be heard from a subjective position, sitting here (just right of the pillar) and heard through acoustic imperfections (my neighbor coughing). And yet this physical specificity is the occasion for an approach to music that foregrounds the transcendence of its physical, objectlike nature, in which these physical origins, while always clearly visible, give way to a musical content defined through a temporal process and an activity of the mind. One uses technology to mask its objectness, from which it never really escapes (because it remains as sensation, not thought); the other is technologically crude, but its object character gives rise to an intellectual activity that transcends its physicality.

Music, like all art, assumes a physical, artifactual quality. That it is a thing is part of the reason we value art at all. In being a thing, an organized whole formed from the interaction of its particular elements by the creative activity of the mind, it redeems the merely thinglike nature of a world of objects that includes ourselves. To use an outmoded language, it spiritualizes objects and thus accomplishes, in miniature, what we consider a definitive human activity. That this object quality of art lends itself to the abuse of a commodity-oriented society is also a central fact of contemporary life. The art object is a paradox: it is an object like any other that seems to dissolve in exchange value, but at the same time it insists on a value that is resistant to exchange value, on being-for-itself. In doing so, it reminds us that other elements of reality (such as people) could also be redeemed in this way.

The fate of music is symptomatic of a social situation far wider than music alone. That our culture is dominated by surfaces, and what one might call a dominant aesthetics of the surface, is evident everywhere. The importance of devoting time, money, and energy to appearances is proclaimed from every billboard and magazine. Consider how often, by comparison, we are accosted about the state of our minds. Viewed from a global perspective, society's collective concern with fitness, diet, exercise regimes, beauty products, and cosmetic surgery is rather peculiar. This concern is not primarily about the basic health of our bodies (we certainly have enough to eat); it is about "quality of life," realizing our potential, feeling as good as we can, and preserving ourselves for as long as we can. But where, one might ask, are the contemporary gymnasia of the mind? Where does one discuss the nutritional value of what we feed our minds? What does it mean that a society cares so little for things of the mind, that art galleries, concert halls, and libraries become increasingly empty while half the population pursues aerobics with a mixture of passion and guilt that was formerly the preserve of the church? This obsession with physicality and appearance extends beyond our bodies and is widely reflected in a culture obsessed by packaging, image, and design. The surface is everything. We live in a visual culture that attaches primary significance to the exchange of signs—of power, attraction, status, wealth, desire—that are overwhelmingly visual. Even in music, visuals are everything: hence the ubiquity not only of the music video but the marketing of the star. And when it comes to the music itself, the surface sheen is everything; the music is literally one-dimensional—it has one sound, one timbre, one kind of material. It rejects polyphony and discursive forms. It is as if the art of costume design were replaced by admiring pieces of cloth, a change of focus that is antithetical to art music, which has always been more concerned with what is done with the material and how it is shaped into meaningful temporal form.

What might seem harmless in relation to cultural practices, fashion, cars, or even music, is clearly invidious in relation to people. The ideal of humanity on which we have based our greatest religious, ethical, philosophical, and political thinking is not defined by our outward, material surface but by our capacity to exceed the limits of our material existence. Great art expresses this ideal in every work. In rejecting it to embrace the ideal of a blank and depthless surface embodied in contemporary culture, we reject that ideal of humanity and instead embrace a simulacrum—a synthetic and hollow substitute. Human potential is not well expressed by the fashionable, the glossy, or the chic, and yet we allow ourselves to be dominated by a culture defined almost exclusively in these terms. In doing so, we collude in our own reduction to objects.

The emphasis on the surface of things is essentially inhumane. It is pornographic because it fetishizes the materiality of human existence and denies the spiritual personality that vivifies it from within. Self-conscious of this fact, it delights in its own debasement in ironic but essentially trapped ways. Perhaps my use of the term "pornographic" seems inappropriate and sensationalist in relation to music. But the central category of pornography is perhaps not sex but the process by which the humane is reduced to the status of things. The theoretical term for this is "reification." Pornography is reification employed in the sexual arena and displays all of its hallmarks: the reproducibility and interchangeability of all commodities, the reduction to an object, the importance of packaging, the reduction to pure surface, the simulacrum of desire, the formulaic sameness of posture, the domination of nature. But the sexual arena does not have a monopoly on the debasement of the humane. While society publicly deplores the objectification of the humane in pornography, it is busy colluding with it elsewhere through advertising, commodity fetishism, and music.

Hegel defined art as the shining forth of a spiritual content through a sensuous form, a definition that mirrors the idea of humanity on which a democratic, individualistic, post-Enlightenment society is built. My use of the term "pornographic" is meant to point to everything that contradicts this fundamental tension by neutralizing what is essentially human to mere materiality, mere objecthood. A culture that is merely sensuous and that denies the activity of the mind within sensuous materials risks becoming pornographic. Dominant culture, I suggest, comes close to this saturation of the materialistic. It is hostile to the intellectual and the genuinely artistic, both of which insist on the human capacity to exceed the material. Art, itself an object, opposes the reduction of the world to things.

Cultural obsession with pure surfaces obscures the technological means that underlie them and make them possible. There is a strange disparity between the sophistication of our technological thinking and the deliberate simplicity of our cultural choices. There is a certain irony in listening to Gregorian plainchant while driving 90 miles per hour in the technological wonders of a new Mercedes. Not only are the two products of such different worlds, but the worldview expressed by one is objectively contradicted by the other. Our obsession with surface seems designed to mask the technological complexity on which it relies. From functional modernism to minimalism, design chic is stripped back and bare. Contemporary pop music demonstrates the same disparity: its computer technology exhibits an unprecedented capacity for the manipulation of sound, and yet the vast majority of the music it serves insists on a primitive, repetitive simplicity. Rock music is rhythmically some of the most impoverished music the world has ever heard, a fact that is hard to square with the sophisticated technologies that produced it.

The history of Western art music, its forms, and its techniques are by no means unrelated to the technological developments of Western societies. Not only are technological changes reflected in musical changes, but music acts as a tracery of the changes the subject undergoes as technology changes the world and our perceptions of it. The degree to which abstract, rational thought has shaped the world we inhabit is encoded in classical music. The rejection of the latter today may have more to do with its modernity than its age. Classical music offends against the insistence on pure surface—it demonstrates its inner workings like a transparent clock face. In the context of a design obsession with surface masking, with the insistence that there is only surface, classical music is embarrassingly earnest and involved: dialectical thought, after all, is horribly awkward and gauche, whereas the absence of thought easily passes for cool. Ironically, for all that youth culture rejects classical music as old-fashioned and out-of-date, it is the way it is because of an excess of rational thought; it is, literally, *too* modern. Instead, youth culture yearns for a prerational immediacy, that of the body, of libidinal energy, and for the luxury of blind, adolescent emotions without consequences or responsibilities. Ironic, too, is that popular culture presents a prerational consciousness as the absolutely modern.

MUSIC AS THOUGHT

We have such a small concept of what thought is or might be. I am not interested in thought *about* music (something that professional musicologists, psychologists, or philosophers might explore). I am interested in thought *in* music, or better, *music as thought*. When you perform a simple piece of arithmetic, you are not thinking *about* mathematics, you are thinking *in* mathematics; mathematics is itself the medium for a certain kind of thought. When you are absorbed in a game such as chess you don't think *about* the game, you think *within* it, and your thought is expressed in terms of the spatial and temporal sequences made available to you by the rules of the game and the state of play on the board. Similarly, when you empathize with another person and act immediately and intuitively on that feeling of empathy, your understanding is not derived from abstract thought on the situation, but rather from a kind of empathetic thinking within the situation. I am suggesting that music invites us to participate in a special kind of thinking that brings together the emotional and intellectual in a uniquely intense and sophisticated manner. That it involves feeling might be unanimously accepted today, although it has by no means always been the prime concern of music or musicians. That it involves thought may strike many people as rather odd, although it has been a central element in the theory, composition, and reception of art music for hundreds of years.

Only in the mind are the evanescent sounds of musical performance held together in a mental construct that outlives the sounds themselves. In this way, music's imprint has an existence out of time. It is not like a recording that we can replay, but it has a unique tone, manner, and form by which we recognize our experience of the musical work. This activity is different both from a purely emotional response to music (though it certainly has a strong element of feeling) and from a purely analytical response to music (though it certainly involves mental differentiation). It differs from the first just as the activity of the wine taster differs from that of someone who drinks to become drunk: its sensitivity to the object is not dulled by becoming lost in one's own response. But at the same time, it is not strictly analytical because it does not distance itself from the object in the way that the analyst must. It does not stand aloof but is carried within the current of the music.

Classical music aspires to the condition of thought because it embodies the basic categories of thought: the differentiation of its materials and their discursive development within a logical sequence. It does this not in imitation of language, as a sublinguistic accompaniment to thinking in words, but rather as an independent and highly sophisticated medium of thought and feeling in its own right. It presents specifically musical ideas through specifically musical forms, elaborated in a way that engages us intellectually, emotionally, and spiritually. Classical music's capacity to unfold a complex discursive whole that engages both the mind and the emotions led to a generation of romantic philosophers and literary figures at the beginning of the nineteenth century seeing music as somehow above and beyond the limits of language. To an age grown skeptical about language's ability to deal adequately with reality, music seemed to present a medium that lost none of the subtlety of linguistic thinking while at the same time avoiding the limitation of concepts. Immanuel Kant, despite his low opinion of music, conceded that art was a kind of thinking without concepts, a "free play" of the cognitive faculties freed from the restrictions of linguistic concepts. It is not insignificant that he expressed this view in 1790, a year before Mozart died and at the height of musical classicism.

At the same time, music is never a purely intellectual exercise: it is irreducibly physical, bodily, and material. It is rooted in the physical world, not only in the vibrations of sounding bodies but in the physiological and psychological effects upon our own bodies and minds. Sound is its most basic requirement, while not itself being music. Music, according to its most basic definition, is not sound but the arrangement of sound. Its specific musical quality (as opposed to the sum of acoustic phenomena) lies in its arrangement, patterning, and form. The diverse musical cultures of the world agree on this point; their primary differentiation is between music and noise, the selection of appropriate sounds for music and the forms by which they are arranged. Of course, sounds and their arrangements are not unrelated; the woodcarver is guided in part by the suggestion of the wood just as the forms developed by architects are inseparable from the physical properties of the materials they employ.

The laws of acoustics do not change: the physical properties of sound are the same for all cultures. What lies behind the huge diversity of music cultures is a huge diversity in how sounds are thought of as music. The production of music as such has always and everywhere been inseparable from thought—from conceiving of sound in certain ways. This is true even of the primary materials of music. Just as a builder does not work with trees and clay but with wood and bricks, so musicians do not work with raw sounds as they are presented "in nature." Music, in all cultures, has its bricks, tiles, beams, bolts; the materials the musician deals with are largely preshaped by their musical culture. When Mozart composed a symphony, he shaped materials that were "common property" of his musical culture: a certain tuning system, scales, melodic and rhythmic patterns, harmonic progressions, phrase structures, musical forms, ensembles for their per-formance, and so on. These materials were already the sediment of a col-lective "thinking" about natural materials, and Mozart's symphony repre-sents the result of a certain creative force shaping those materials. In this way, the musical work is the result of a twofold mediation of its acoustic materials—the first by a musical culture as a whole, the second by the in-dividual composer. Of course, that we seem to experience music "imme-diately" is apt to mask the depth of this cultural mediation.

All music is grounded in a balance between the physical nature of sounds and the work of the mind upon sounds. Musical traditions are de-fined not only by different musical materials, but by different ways of thinking about them. What distinguishes the classical or art-music tradi-tion from other musics is a particular way of thinking about musical ma-terials and the forms into which they are shaped. Consider rhythm, for ex-ample. Music's "beat" is often seen as its most basic, elemental aspect. The maintenance of a regular pulse or beat might seem universal of all musics until one reflects on a range of solo vocal and instrumental genres that have a free, improvisational approach to rhythmic groupings. One might at least contend that a regular beat is universal to all dance music, that this most physical aspect of music is required to elicit the most obviously phys-ical response to music—dancing. But in classical music, rhythm is rarely defined by beat alone: beat or pulse is merely an empty temporal grid upon which the patternings of divisions and additions of rhythm are projected. Musical tone presents a similar case. A single tone, or a collection of tones, is rarely a musical entity in itself; melody arises from the patterning of tones, by both pitch and rhythm. The melody is as much the pattern as it is the sound—arguably more so, since we carry the melody with us long after the sound has ceased.

That music originates from and is expressed through the human body is not in dispute. But if myth suggests that music began in the bodily realm— in song and in dance—the desire to make music with other objects is likely just as ancient. The desire to draw musical sound from inert objects, made or found, appears to have developed with the desire to make music with one's own body. Instrumental music has often maintained a close relationship to the bodily both in design (witness the "torso" design of the guitar or cello) and in the fact that instrumental melody often relates to the sound and patterns of the human singing voice. At the same time, the specific value of instrumental music derives from its capacity for transcending the limitations of the human body: instruments can play faster, higher, and lower and can make wider leaps than the human voice. Some instruments can sound several notes at once and never need to breathe. A musical instrument is thus "instrumental" in a broader sense: it is the tool or vehicle by which we transcend the limitations of our bodies.

Most musical traditions exhibit a balance between the vocal (rooted in the immediacy of the body) and the instrumental (exceeding the immediate through technology). Classical music may not be unique in its emphasis on autonomous instrumental music, but the predominance of instrumental forms is a distinguishing feature. The rise of autonomous music in the eighteenth century, music that was not ancillary to other activities, was bound up with instrumental music. Most of all, it was bound up with the development of keyboard instruments and the piano. The keyboard embodied an abstract rationalization of musical sound that has shaped Western music ever since. Not only does it present a disembodied voice (what one strikes is not what makes the noise); it also presents an unprecedented simultaneity of possibilities. One person can produce several voices with this instrument. To look at the keyboard is to see all the notes at the same time, suggesting for the first time the vertical simultaneity of harmony, as opposed to harmony arising from the coincidence of horizontal lines. The keyboard initiated the spatialization of music. Moreover, it laid out the continuum of musical pitch in the discretely tuned scale (something strings and voices still moved in and out of). And its voices were instantly balanced. It spoke in several voices but with uniform tone; it was the perfect ensemble. The keyboard was also central to a change in the social space of music, from communal and public spaces such as the church or court to domestic and private spaces. Just as the new space for music emphasized an inward and private, self-reflective activity, so keyboard music was differentiated from the more bodily functions of singing and dancing.

The differentiation of musical materials is by no means limited to the development of instrumental genres—the complexities of renaissance choral music are self-evident. Historically, however, the elaboration of more discursive musical forms, such as the sonata, the symphony, and the classical concerto, took place in purely instrumental genres. The precondition of these more discursive forms is a high degree of musical differentiation. Characteristically, classical works present materials that seem to require further elaboration or extension through development or variation before being rounded out to a close that seems to balance and reconcile its various elements. It is not that classical music lacks closed lyrical forms, but it tends to work from the part to the whole and to fashion large-scale formal resolutions through the successive patterning of harmonic dissonance. In this way it resembles the novel and the philosophical treatise. It shares with them an unfolding through successive events, interruptions, deductions, consequences, and elaborations, while doing all of this with materials that may seem as abstract as the materials of nonrepresentational art. Classical works rarely tell stories, but they often unfold like a story or drama. Engaging with the work requires following the unfolding of difference and the subtle changes in character, mood, pace, attitude, tone, and bearing, as well as sudden events that threaten the work's coherence, right through to the denouement and resolution. Classical music does not literally tells stories, but its unfolding depends on similar narrative devices of character, transformation, development, interaction, anticipation, recall, pacing, and plot.

Music's discursive character operates in several ways. The tone is often narrational: sometimes theatrical, it makes grand opening gestures similar to the raising of a curtain, or establishes a mood prior to the main character's arrival. Elsewhere, the music is more intimate; it hints at what is to come or what has already passed. But the unfolding is also narrational in that the music progresses by a series of events and characters; ideas are introduced and discussed as motivic fragments are passed between different instrumental voices. Chamber music often has this quality of interaction between its plural voices, discursive and emotional at the same time. These plural voices are both literal and figurative. A solo piano piece can speak polyphonically, and an orchestral piece can speak as a collective unison. Either way, the multiple voices constitute a distinctive aspect. The work coheres by interweaving voices that at times are at odds with one another, that disagree and contradict as well as support and complement. The same unfolding process mirrors the thought process, a discursive interaction and resolution that involves both intellect and feeling. It mirrors the process of negotiation, development, and exchange by which we are extended as individuals—through self-reflective thought, through the expansion of our consciousness, through our collective negotiations with others.

This is not a vague analogy or metaphor, nor does music link to these things because it stimulates us to think about them. Music unfolds in a temporal process similar to the process of our own self-development. Thus, the polyphonic lines of a piece unfold in the larger harmonic framework that is responsible for the large-scale tension and resolution of the music. This is a major difference between the dynamic forms of classical music and the static forms of other musical traditions. Static forms have no concept of structural dissonance, being based essentially on repetition and variation. Classical music may not encapsulate our whole being, but it does offer a unique musical vehicle for the dynamic aspect of an autonomous, self-developing subjectivity. If our subjectivity is defined between a sense of being and becoming, this is the very tension classical music reworks. We do not experience ourselves in an utterly static way, but through an essential tension between the immediacy of our being and our potential to be other, a tension encoded in our basic perception of time as divided into past and future. Classical music has been concerned with the patterning of these temporal tensions from Monteverdi to Mozart, from Beethoven to Boulez.

THE CROSSING OF LIMITS

I have suggested that music's capacity to function as art is defined by the way it embodies a kind of thinking within specifically musical categories. As music it remains rooted in its own physical medium—that of sound— but also projects a content beyond mere sound by its patterning of these elements. Music-as-art thus exceeds the conditions of its medium, just as literature amounts to more than words. But music's medium is not just sound; it is also time. Music does not just take place in time, in the literal sense of its duration; its patterns of repetition, transformation, recall, and anticipation shape our experience of time. It offers modalities of temporal experience different from those of everyday life—often uniquely intense experiences at that. Musical time is not the same as external, clock time; music interiorizes time and thus has a freedom in its organization of time not possible in everyday life. It can exceed the usual boundaries that time appears to exhibit. Music can construct a familiar sense of temporal progression toward the future, but it can also recall past events or dwell on future events as if they were already present. It can accelerate the passage of time or slow it down until all forward motion seems to be suspended and music simply "floats."

This is neither a technical trick nor merely the projection of our responses onto the music: it is, once again, the result of the music's objective patterning of its materials. Its progressions and sequences of motivic and harmonic materials construct metaphors of corresponding temporal progression and sequence, but it can also interrupt these with flashbacks to earlier moments or anticipations of later events. This can be heard in the music of many composers. Consider, for example, the third movement of Mahler's Ninth Symphony, in which a tempestuous musical argument is repeatedly interrupted by momentary premonitions of the resolution to come in the fourth and final movement.

Music has a particularly powerful link to subjective experience. It relates directly to the experience of our subjectivity because it mirrors the way our own sense of identity is established through time, by the persistence of defining features across time and their synthesis into a complex unity. We recognize in music's temporal unfolding the internal narratives of our selves, a tracery of the same patterns that seem to define our emotional, psychological, and spiritual experience. More than this, music can project a patterning of its materials that exceeds our immediate experience, offering us the experience of internal narratives, or musical journeys, that are not our own. In other words, we experience in music what we cannot experience outside of it. It structures time and identity in ways that we find intensely fulfilling precisely because they are not those of everyday life.

This reformulation of time and identity, the crossing of boundaries impossible in everyday life, is one of the most significant values of music as it is of art more generally. Music provides us with an immediate experience that seems to reflect on itself within its unfolding process. In this way, it surely mirrors a crucial aspect of our complex experience of ourselves in time. Different musics undoubtedly do this in different ways and to varying degrees. Some emphasize the pure immediacy of the present moment; others are far more discursive and put off the fullness of the present with long-range, future-oriented structures. They relate to different aspects of ourselves and different conceptions of ourselves. That we are defined by plural and competing voices, that we are always multiple selves, is perhaps best captured in music whose multiple voices reflect this.

Classical music is multiple in several ways. To some extent, for example, the sequence of movements of a sonata or symphony reflects different aspects of the self, different ways of being—a discursive first movement being followed by a more lyrical slow movement. But single movements also contain this multiplicity, often opposing contrasting materials that the music seeks to integrate through juxtaposition, variation, and transformation. Polyphony, the simultaneous combination of several voices or lines, expresses this fundamental multiplicity integrated into a single unity. Singing a Renaissance mass by Victoria or Lassus, or a baroque fugue by Bach or Handel, one is part of a complex collective whole in which no single voice dominates: the interaction of the separate voices embodies a musical analogue of the perfectly balanced community, and no doubt it served as such in its original religious setting.

Later uses of polyphony, in the nineteenth and twentieth centuries, for example, have often been seen as expressive not so much of the ideal of community but of the complex competing voices of the self. The plural lines of a Mahler symphony or a Schoenberg string quartet thus come to illustrate the complex divided modern self. For some, the music of the classical period proper, of Haydn, Mozart, and Beethoven, provides a unique balance of both claims, mediating those of the collective and those of the individual. The boundary between the two is perhaps the most important of those boundaries of external life that music is uniquely placed to reformulate and transgress. In music there is no literal border between inner and outer, private and public, individual and collective, and yet music mediates these dualities in all sorts of ways. Opera, itself an invention of the age of individualism initiated by the Renaissance, makes this opposition explicit and thematic; indeed, the alternation of outward public action and inward private reflection provides an underlying structural pattern for opera. But instrumental music, too, has its ways of demarcating modalities of outward and inward voices.

This essential aspect of music needs to be reasserted in the face of a crude classification of music that makes folk and popular styles collective where classical music is solitary. Classical music is written by (famously) solitary individuals, whereas the creation of popular music is associated more with groups; the classical listener may sit in a concert hall with others, but he or she remains isolated by physical immobility and silence, whereas the collective participation in popular music almost always involves direct interaction with others. And yet even the most solitary musical activity (like a shepherd piping alone in the mountains, or someone playing the piano in an empty house) enacts a certain collective participation, because even solo music, simply through speaking a collective language, is a means of negotiating the relationship of the individual to the collective. Of course, the performance of music is usually a collective activity and, irrespective of the kind of music involved or even whether it is live or recorded, it seems to bind performers, listeners, dancers, and even bystanders together in a collective activity that presumes varying degrees of collective experience.

Music is always the mediation of individuality and collectivity: it reformulates the borders between the two by repeatedly transgressing them in its own internal language. But it does this in different ways. There is a difference between the outward collective activity that arises from music's performative aspect and the way music mediates the relationship of individual and collective in its own process. Unison hymn singing, for example, embodies a unity of collective statement quite different from that of an improvisation group. Less dramatically, the harmonized chorales in Bach's choral music mediate the relation of individual and collective differently than the contrapuntal, often fugal movements of the same works. A symphony orchestra implies a social collectivity even when used to articulate what seems highly personal and subjective music.

Classical music of the late eighteenth century strove for a collective identity, but one generated by the productive activity of the individual, thus embodying in musical form an Enlightenment ideal of subjective freedom. The historical path from this position to modernism may be understood as the struggle to maintain that balance in an increasingly impersonal society, so that the individual is compelled to exaggerate its subjective moment. The much talked about "alienation" (which binds romanticism to modernism) is this sense of rupture between self-identity and individuals' place in the collective. The affirmation of classical music became harder to square with the objective changes to musical language that took place in the nineteenth century. Classical music thus became increasingly suspicious of a collectivity that was too immediately achieved. This is one important reading of the divergence of popular and art music from the end of the nineteenth century onward. Art was more and more preoccupied with the authenticity of a subject that was not bound to an immediate collectivity and found the simple affirmation of popular culture facile, superficial, and ultimately false. For its part, popular culture was popular precisely because it fulfilled the basic need to affirm a collectivity by making the image in culture of a collectivity that did not exist in society. Modernist art music, in contrast, has been judged sterile, impersonal, and unremittingly negative—if not elitist in its inability to speak in a common tongue—for refusing this fundamental solace.

For many people, classical music seems like a solitary activity, not just in its production but also in its reception. Performers on stage behave in highly formalized ways and seem to interact with one another very little.

Audiences, even when they are large, show virtually no collective activity except the simple, ritualistic act of applause. But anyone who has sung in a large choir, elevated behind a symphony orchestra, would find this hard to understand. To sing a line doubled by fifty other singers in a choral symphony made of several such overlapping strands and performed by several hundred people is quite literally to exceed one's boundaries and become part of a larger polyphonic whole. Similarly, the members of a string quartet or even a singer-pianist duo know well that *through the music* they engage in a collectivity that exceeds their individual contributions.

The difference between the formal, even ritualized behavior surrounding classical music and other kinds of tradition hinges on classical music's attitude toward the body, which relates to ideas of both collectivity and immediacy. Outwardly, classical music appears highly repressed. Its dress codes, body language, restraint, and formality all seem to point to a denial of the bodily. Above all, the image of the classically trained listener, sitting silent and immobile throughout the performance, would suggest that classical music shuns the immediacy of bodily expression. People do not dance in the aisles at classical concerts. This is an important difference, and ample evidence that classical music and popular traditions simply *do* different things. But classical music is based not so much on a denial of the body as on a different balance between its bodily and nonbodily elements. Much classical music is rooted in the bodily but aims at transcending, without denying, those physical origins. Purely instrumental music, whether by Bach, Haydn, or Stravinsky, often makes clear its derivation from the more bodily forms of dance and song. Classical music comes from the body but is about being more than the body: it enacts the quitting of the body through the bodily— hence its fundamentally ritualistic, mythical power, representing in the physicality of the body our spiritual aspiration to be more than bodies.

Consider J. S. Bach's *Goldberg Variations*. The theme of this work is an aria—that is to say, a song. And although the aria here is played entirely on the keyboard, it nevertheless implies the attributes of vocal expression—of words, the voice, and thus the body. But Bach's work is for the most abstract musical instrument, the keyboard, and his thirty variations are similarly "supravocal." An idea is thus presented in its concrete materiality (the melody of the aria) but then elaborated in a seemingly infinite play, transcending what is immediately given. When the aria theme is repeated at the end of the cycle it is to affirm that all of this play is contained within a union of mind and body, matter and spirit. Indeed, such dualities are never made within the music. This piece comes close to the notion we have of ourselves—as a unified whole, self-identical, not diffused but infinitely diversified, expanding, creative, subtle, sensitive. To play the aria alone, as would certainly happen in a contemporary compilation of classical excerpts, is to make it one-dimensional compared to the vast expansion that the work as a whole achieves. That expansion is an activity of the mind or spirit: its central characteristic is that it exceeds the objectlike nature of the simple song while also redeeming it. It is a model of what classical music does to its material: not denying it but redeeming it by demonstrating that it is always more, that its nature lies in its dynamic potential to become something other.

Similarly, consider almost any movement from the suites for solo cello or partitas for solo violin by J. S. Bach. Most dramatically of all, when Bach writes a fugue for solo violin, he quite literally exceeds the limits of the instrument and its single player. The idea of the single singing voice carried by the violin is transcended by this extension toward polyphony. Through the performer's enactment the music realizes the spiritual aspiration of a baroque consciousness: the expansion of the individual into a choric proliferation. One could rewrite the music for three separate instruments, or realize it electronically, to facilitate the articulation of the different lines. But either of these acts would utterly miss the music's fundamental point: the transgression of the limits of a single player, and with it, the proposing of a human spirit and creativity that also transcend their physical limits.

Art mediates our experience of the world and of ourselves by dealing with limits, boundaries, and borders in a way that real life rarely allows. Not only is art often concerned with the outer limits of our experience; it is often concerned with the limits of its own expressive capacities. Art claims a unique capacity for representing and enacting the transgression of limits. It defines limits through its discursive logic, which it transgresses even as it presents them. In this, it articulates a fundamental human aspiration; in the activity of its thinking, it goes beyond its material individuality. It projects a symbolic meaning through the patterning of its materials without obliterating their particularity. In this way art accomplishes its primary goal: to recreate the world, to transform it in the crucible of human creativity.

Art thus suggests that the world is, or could be, something other than we take it to be. It invites a reorientation, a change of perspective. This is not necessarily an aesthetic of modernist or overtly challenging art. It is the challenge of all art worthy of the name. Mozart, for example, possesses this quality in abundance even though, superficially, his musical language seems overfamiliar and even though his music is often associated with the reproduction and reinforcement of the status quo. Mozart's music exhibits greater radical potential than plenty of more recent music because of its dialogue between limitation and transgression. This is an objective feature of the musical text: musical limits are established only to be crossed. It can be objectively demonstrated in terms of its deployment of harmony, phrase structure, form, and so on. This music offers the continual possibility of being other, of making the world other. Its vitality lies in the sense of infinite possibility, in the idea that what is proposed may not be produced, that things may turn out differently yet still coherently. It is not simply ungrounded fantasy, but rather the infinite possibilities of imagination and human spirit in tension with the objective confrontation with reality. This is inscribed in the musical language and form: its form is precisely such a dialogue. Of course, one can miss all this; one can hear only the repetition of old formulas in Mozart's music. But then one can equally fail to make sense of Shakespeare's use of the English language or find the elegance of a mathematical equation so much nonsense.

Classical music is more concerned with the *process* of subjectivity than with a position statement, more interested in the process of identity formation than in the definition of any single, static identity. It explores these matters by maintaining a very particular balance between the physicality of its sonic materials and the intellectual activity through which they are transformed and patterned. Being both physical and intellectual, classical music enacts the repeated exceeding of one by the other that is a condition of being fully human. Those elements strike us together: there is no separation between the physical and the intellectual. Classical music becomes marginal in contemporary culture precisely because it refuses such a dualistic division. Contemporary culture tends toward a polarization in which the intellectual, reflective activity of the mind is marginalized; it thus becomes the activity of the eccentric—peripheral, unvalued, and slightly comical. What society really values, as the popular media confirm daily, is an ideal of being human represented by pure visuality undisturbed by the awkward questioning of the intellect. Classical music, like the activity of the mind more generally, is too articulate to be cool.

Art music does not jettison the bodily in order to enter a realm of pure thought; it is neither sonic philosophy nor acoustic math. Its essence is to project a pattern of thought and feeling through the patterning of its sounding, physical elements. The spiritual element of music is therefore not some mystical essence or secret ingredient that genius composers add and we receive through a process of transubstantiation. It is there for the taking because it arises from the patterning, the form of material elements. It does what we are all capable of doing: by thinking the material elements of the world, it spiritualizes them. In this way, such a music projects a content that is essentially humane.

CHAPTER 4. UNDERSTANDING MUSIC

ADULT LITERACY

The ability to read and write is fundamental to adult life. Understanding the world around us and being able to express our thoughts and feelings through the written word is considered basic. It is understood as a right to which all adults should have access: a right that not only concerns the personal development of individuals, but forms the very basis of a modern democratic society. A democracy presumes literacy in such a way that it becomes not only the right of its members but, effectively, a requirement and a responsibility.

When children learn to read, they acquire skills through a carefully graded path. They gradually learn not only new vocabulary but more complicated grammatical constructions. Educational curricula are based on the notion of "reading ages," and the books children read at different stages of their education reflect these in style, format, and content. We take great care to ensure that reading material is appropriate for our children and that it helps ·them develop a mature understanding of themselves and the world. Indeed, we link maturity and intelligence so closely to literacy that adults who have never learned to read or write must deal with considerable stigma. We would be alarmed if our children grew up without progressing beyond the books they read in elementary school or if they could deal only with texts in comic book format. Why? Because we believe that the development of literacy is central to the full development of an adult, that it enables a greater participation in social life, a richer experience of the world, and an enhancement of one's capacity for self-expression; without it, we seem to lack a vital tool for fulfilling our social potential.

While such views are generally held, we frequently ignore the principles by and for which our children are educated. Much of the literature we consume requires the ability to read in only the most basic sense and in no way exercises a more developed literary sense or the critical tools we aspire to teach our children at school. Even less are we required in adult life to exercise our abilities for self-expression in writing. The majority of tabloid journalism, magazines, and best-selling novels assume both a low reading age and a short attention span. What differentiates them from texts aimed at children is simply the mode of presentation and the subject matter.

Why does contemporary culture exhibit this lack of differentiation between children's and adults' literacy? Why does the majority of adult culture require little more sophistication of understanding than children's culture? As we have seen, mainstream contemporary culture does not make this distinction and tends to blur the cultural definition of adults and children. This cuts both ways: we see children appropriating the accoutrements of adult life, and we also see adults' desire to take on aspects of youth culture. That adults are often content with a musical culture shaped primarily around children is an odd phenomenon, one that we would question in other areas of our life. It suggests that we do not regard our musical literacy in the same way as we do reading and that we are untroubled by the idea of a "reading age" in relation to music.

But if, in general, our musical literacy remains relatively undeveloped, there is little enthusiasm for rectifying this. Most people would fiercely resist the idea that they need any instruction in how to listen to music. Because we can hear, we think we can listen. But just because we can see, we don't assume we can read. Reading means gaining familiarity with shared social conventions so that we can understand how literary texts work. There is a strong element of objectivity in this. The alphabet is not up for debate, nor is the difference between a verb and a noun or the basic uses of the period. So why the resistance in the case of music? To play football you have to know the rules, and to play it well you may have to practice a long time. So why, with music, potentially one of our most sophisticated mediums of thought, does the idea of learning seem so ridiculous? This question leads into deep waters. Music is private, personal, immediate, instinctive, unconscious; it is beyond the bounds of academic analysis and the scrutiny of reflective thought.

Where music survives in formal education, it has of necessity shifted its focus over the last generation to mirror everyday culture rather than to reflect *upon* it. One begins with the everyday musical experience of students, not something that is completely alien to them. Too often, perhaps, one ends there, too. It would be incomprehensible to teach a foreign language this way, or science, or even English literature. This is not to say that new things cannot be related to students' own experience, but surely a fundamental goal of education is to extend the view and the grasp, to both challenge and develop confidence to cope with those challenges.

Music education has become a contested field because it is the site of a central debate about cultural values and authority. Education is authoritarian in the sense that it is selective and therefore judgmental, not so much about students but about the materials it foregrounds as of greater significance than others. As such, it is a central means of cultural legitimation and, potentially, cultural critique, which is why education is never politically neutral. But though education is selective, it is not a closed system: it is the site of dispute, contestation, and negotiation. A balanced music education would certainly place Western art music in relation to other traditions, both non-Western and popular. But to do so as if these were so many consumer choices—simply a matter of personal preference—is to seriously mislead. Understanding musical differences involves understanding where musics come from and what they say. It means being literate, therefore, in musical languages. Presenting children with musical styles in which they are not literate is a little like presenting them with poems in languages they do not speak. If they reject Bach or Verdi or Bartók in preference for the Beatles or Robbie Williams, isn't that similar to rejecting poems in German, Italian, or Hungarian in preference for those in English? And if this is so, doesn't the expression of preference have nothing to do with the intrinsic qualities of the music or poetry and everything to do with familiarity?

Our resistance to treating music as something requiring work is deep-seated. In the nineteenth century, music's subjective element was emphasized to the extent that the apparently "ruleless" freedom of the composer eventually became the domain of the listener, too. Everything seemed to be about personal, subjective, and private response. The twentieth century has seen a reaction (at least among some composers and academics) against this unbridled subjectivity of popular listening, insisting on the objectivity of the musical text. Recently, this has shown signs of relenting, not least because in overstating the case and forgetting that an abstract idea of music and its actual reception are not equivalent, this position has become slightly ridiculous. But in this to-ing and fro-ing, any balance to the equation has been hopelessly obscured.

Art does not lack immediacy. There are numerous examples of classical works making an immediate and powerful impact on audiences that were surprised to be so affected. Puccini's aria "Nessun Dorma," popularized by "The Three Tenors"; Auden's poem "Stop all the clocks," popularized by the film *Four Weddings and a Funeral*; Mozart's *Requiem* in the film *Amadeus*—all of these suggest that, given a different context, classical works can have an immediate and powerful effect. For many people, some of their most intense and memorable experiences of music are associated with such initial encounters, perhaps at a time in their lives when their wider knowledge of genre, tradition, and language was still at an elementary stage. Expert knowledge certainly does not equate with intensity of experience; indeed, it often reduces it. My point is that art's specific and distinctive claim rests on something beyond its immediate potency and that a richer understanding of it involves a sensitivity to its formal properties that goes beyond its immediate emotional effect. A vibrant performance of Shakespeare (films included) can affect an audience untutored in Elizabethan literature, just as a vibrant performance of a Beethoven or Mahler symphony can. But to read Eliot or Joyce, to listen to the music of Debussy or Berg, requires a literacy that extends beyond the immediacy of innocent first impressions.

This is an unpopular idea. The notion of literacy is rejected as part of the elitist baggage surrounding art and music, a final barrier policed by academics and experts now that many of the economic ones have fallen. The demand for immediacy has the ring of a popular politics, just as the demand for literacy has the whining tone of an ousted elite, a mean-spirited caviling that concedes the citadels may have been stormed but that their contents will never be "understood" by an illiterate mass audience. In Britain, these opposing positions have been neatly marked in the differences between two competing radio stations, the publicly funded BBC Radio 3 and the commercial Classic FM. Radio 3's traditional approach implies that the understanding of a musical work is enhanced by knowledge about it, whereas Classic FM's approach implies that great music speaks directly and immediately. Music that requires some sort of verbal commentary is thus, almost by definition, rather weak.

Audience figures alone demonstrate that many people find this approach refreshing and compelling. But as Classic FM's playlist reveals, it is tied up with classical music functioning as popular music. Most striking, quite apart from the difference in presentational tone and other framing devices, is what is *not* played on Classic FM: anything that risks being less than popular. This includes not only "difficult" modern music but also earlier music deemed too serious or heavy. Even well-represented composers' works are usually given as extracts; one hears arias rather than operas, movements rather than symphonies. And one hears certain works over and over—the result of the commercial chart system applied to classical pieces.

By contrast, the traditional rationale behind Radio 3 is essentially educative, a position that is either enlightened and benign or patriarchal and elitist, depending on your point of view. Of course, some of the music is the same as that broadcast by Classic FM, but it is framed quite differently.

Not only will Radio 3 most likely play the whole work, but its presenters have traditionally prefaced it with historical and even analytical information, implying that its claim to be art music hinges on more than its immediate effect. The contrast in ratings between the two stations suggests that this position, for all its high ideals, is not very popular.

This situation makes clear that for most of its audience, classical music is enjoyed as part of popular culture; that is to say, it is enjoyed for its immediate effect on the listener. Radio 3 smacks too much of school, with its implication that certain canonical texts have to be wrestled with, no matter how difficult, and that education and personal pleasure are never directly commensurate. This is related to the uses we expect music to fulfill, a question that turns on our almost universal division of work and leisure. But it also has to do with our education, which was surely lacking if it did not give us the ability to derive rich and rewarding experiences from things that were initially unappealing.

READING AND MISREADING

The act of listening is not literally an act of reading; a better pair of terms might be "hearing" and "mishearing." When I mishear someone and thus misunderstand them, the problem may be cognitive rather than aural, hinging on the fact that I am unable to decode what they have said. I can hear their voice perfectly, but I miss what is said, perhaps because they speak with a strong, unfamiliar accent. This kind of commonsense position is a necessary counterweight to the theoretical positions of literary and cultural theory, the most extreme of which seem to accord such significance to the subjective act of reception that the claims of the object or text are all but lost. While it is true that meanings change, it is equally true that they are not arbitrary. Our continued belief in the communicative power of language and of culture more generally rests on our acknowledgment that the text or object has certain objective properties, is structured in certain ways, and is not infinitely open to arbitrary interpretation.

Living in a culture requires that we understand broadly agreed-upon symbolic conventions. To speak of culture at all presumes that meaning has a validity beyond individual interpretations. Meaning that is defined purely by the individual has nothing to do with the idea of culture. This relationship, between subjective expression and social meaning, is rooted in language, with its tension between the social demands of language and the individual speech acts through which we enter into it. To take part in a collective culture means acknowledging the difference between what is meant by "fish" and "love," just as it means recognizing that a red traffic light does not mean "Go" and understanding that my neighbor's friendly smile is not an invitation to sexual intercourse.

Artworks do not employ precise symbolic languages, like math, nor are they linguistic propositions in the everyday sense. Nevertheless, they exhibit certain objective features. Hamlet's soliloquy does not begin with the words "To flee or not to flee," nor does Beethoven's Fifth Symphony begin with a saxophone solo. While Hamlet's soliloquy may be open to interpretation, its meaning is not infinitely adaptable. I can, however, misread and thus misunderstand it. A combination of unfamiliarity with Elizabethan vocabulary and syntax on the one hand and carelessness and lack of reflection on the other might lead me to hear something the text has not said. I have the right to do this, to enjoy *Hamlet* in my own private fashion, but this has little to do with *Hamlet* and nothing to do with culture.

Music, of course, appears to be far less definitive a text, especially if we rule out the score and concentrate on music as sound. Without a highly technical descriptive language, music is notoriously difficult to discuss in a detailed and collectively meaningful way. When people do talk about music (rather than performance), they almost always focus on their responses to it rather than on the music itself. But it is by no means impossible to do the latter: to be able to refer to "the bit where the horns play that fanfare" or "the very quiet, slow ending" hardly requires years of technical study. We recognize features of music as we recognize features of visual art, without necessarily knowing exactly how they were composed or having a technical language for describing them.

Technical language is, in any case, a mixed blessing. Too often it has nothing to do with understanding the work and everything to do with summarizing its ingredients and the plan by which it was put together. To talk of keys and motifs may get us no closer to understanding the work than to talk about burnt ochre or cobalt blue in painting. Nevertheless, such things do refer to objective features of the work. It may not matter that I lack the vocabulary to identify a move to D major, but it may be deeply significant that I am receptive to that moment in the piece when the music's ambiguity of the last few minutes is suddenly replaced by something clear and unambiguous.

Consider, for example, the transition from the scherzo to the finale of Beethoven's Fifth Symphony. To draw on inadequate and bland metaphors, this passage ascends from dark, musical depths to a moment of clear arrival and energetic affirmation. To say as much, however inadequately put, is more than a matter of opinion or personal perception: it constitutes a culturally literate judgment, like recognizing that a particular deployment of paint represents a cultural ideal of the Madonna or that

Hamlet's soliloquy in act 3 constitutes an existential question. The ability to talk in technical terms about the Beethoven example does not necessarily imply a greater understanding. To talk of the move from C minor to C major, the chromatic movement over the sustained dominant pedal, the change of meter, and the transition from obscure to clearly defined timbres does not of itself point to any greater understanding than that possessed by listeners who hear these things without naming them but who are fully responsive to what they add up to. And it may well be that such listeners who neither name the musical phenomena nor project onto the piece their own emotional narratives nevertheless understand the music more fully in that moment of response, a moment of unconscious recognition that the music, through this arrangement of its materials, makes a link to wider, homologous phenomena: the breaking up of dark storm clouds and the sudden reappearance of the sun, or the dispersal of profound doubt and anxiety by the unexpected emergence of a clear answer.

I am being deliberately crude. Some will be alienated by such a simplistic description, others by what seems to be a ridiculous and arbitrary projection onto the music of my own program. Such is the gap between how we understand these things. Music is not reducible, of course, to such poetic metaphors, but neither is it unrelated to them. Those who employ the technical language of musical analysis do so to avoid reducing musical meaning, to close down its multivalent significance by the projections of the listener, but this approach risks losing sight of why musical patternings and forms are meaningful at all. One can mishear the music. If one fails to register this moment in Beethoven's Fifth (or hears it in opposite terms), that does not constitute merely a difference of opinion or personal interpretation; it constitutes a mishearing or misreading of the music—a degree of cultural illiteracy akin to imagining that "fish" means "love," that a red light means "Go," or that every smile is an invitation to sexual intercourse.

While we concede the objectivity of judgments in other cultural areas, in music we cling stubbornly to the authority of individual feeling and intuition. We insist that no response is more valid or authoritative than another. Indeed, to many, the very idea of authority in relation to musical understanding (as opposed to knowledge *about* music) is complete anathema. It offends the principle of our pseudo-democracy, in which "art for all" implies that one also accords equality to everyone's opinion about art. The authority of "the expert" is resented because it appears to be based on something that can neither be produced as evidence nor proven. Just as the work of art is incomprehensible to someone with no knowledge of the culture in which it is produced, so too is one's understanding related to one's familiarity with that culture. In other words, artworks derive their cultural meaning partly from the context of other works in which they are made. It is this broader cultural knowledge that the expert claims, finding in the intertextuality of hundreds of works the basis for advancing a particular interpretation of the single work in question.

A piece of music is no different in this than a poem or painting. To understand a poem, one has to be literate not only in language but also, generally speaking, in the formal conventions of the poetic genre and the broader tradition of poetry. One can misunderstand a poem in gross ways (not knowing the meaning of a word or failing to follow an archaic grammatical construction) and in subtle ways (failing to sense the resonance of references and allusions). But with poetry and painting, there seems to be firmer ground for dispute over meaning. Both employ mediums whose reference to ideas and things is more specific and more widely agreed upon. In classical instrumental music, as is often insisted, meaning is apparently intrinsically musical and self-referential. Moreover, the medium is understood more in the highly subjective realm of emotions than in the collectively disputable realm of rational intellect. Few people would deny that music lends itself to a breadth of personal experience and understanding that often exceeds that of language, but we are more likely to agree on the meaning a poem than a sonata.

This difficulty is compounded by the belief that what is meaningful and valuable about music should be given to us *immediately*. Indeed, the immediacy of musical experience is one of the prime reasons we value it. To many, the idea that music or art more generally should have "hidden depths" is simply the pretension of intellectuals and modern artists. Contemporary popular culture has no time for this: art should appeal directly to the individual, and it should have an immediate effect. Art that seems to require reflection or intellectual commentary is either irrelevant or simply bad.

Yet immediacy cannot be a criteria for art. In order to enter a work, to engage with musical discourse on its own terms rather than merely responding to its surface signs, we have to go beyond immediacy. When turning a radio dial and catching brief moments of music, we can often place those musical styles as easily as the different languages we hear. But by the same token, these snippets often have no more meaning for us. As we turn the dial, we understand not the words' content but the signs of Germanness, Frenchness, Dutchness, and so forth. Not being fluent in these languages, we might be none the wiser if we continued to listen to one channel rather than moving on. The same might be said of the music we come across. We hear the signs of classical, jazz, disco, country, Asian, and no more. This is, of course, how background music works. Sitting in a restaurant for two hours, one takes from the music only a sense of "Indianness" or "classical."

This changes the moment we actively engage with the music, a moment akin to opening a book rather than being mesmerized by its cover. Active engagement is no guarantee of understanding, but it is a precondition. Of course, we remain free to use art music as a sign for other things, but to work as art it requires us to engage with it on its own terms, in the details of its materials and their formal patterning. To speak its language fluently requires an immersion that our lives often seem to preclude. But the moment we enter into the work, rather than dwelling on its immediate effect upon us, we have to respond to what the work gives us. Things happen in artworks: things are done and said. Understanding the artwork means playing along, which is quite impossible if one treats what is done and said as arbitrary, as simply a matter of personal response.

Artworks, music included, are extremely precise in what they say and do, but they are precise in their own terms. The musical statement at the beginning of a Mozart symphony is unequivocal, and the way that statement is repeated, commented upon, and argued is precise and explicit even though it refuses any kind of paraphrase or translation into nonmusical terms. Engaging in art means engaging in specific details of what it says and does, just as engaging in dialogue with another person does. Art "happens" when we allow ourselves to take part in a dialogue with it, when we allow ourselves to follow the things it says and does—when we play along.

The demands art makes on us are neither determined by us nor arbitrary. They are made by the art object itself. What it says can be misread, but no amount of misreading changes the object. If I listen to a traditional Chinese song, I may respond to the music after a fashion. It may evoke a complex bundle of associations of ancient China: tall, misty mountain landscapes, poems about cherry blossoms and the new moon, poignant sadness amid the beauty of autumn. Suppose this song, however, actually extolled the fine qualities of Chinese tractors and other agricultural machinery in the People's Republic. Those who argue that music's meaning is simply that which the listener invests it with, and that this experience is as valid as any other, would suggest that my misreading does not matter. That, the argument runs, is the meaning of the song *to me*.

If we are to talk of culture at all, that is simply nonsense. Culture is not about what the work means to me; it is about the meaning the work has *beyond* my immediate response and how I position my response in relation to that larger meaning. Just as I can misread your words or your smile, a road sign, or even the weather, I can misread music. Music is not denotational in a linguistic way, but neither is it wholly abstract. It is not a direct representation of other things, but neither is it divorced from the world in which it is made. It offers significant experience because it arises from a significant process of formation, shaped by a myriad of significant creative decisions. Anyone who has created anything knows that these decisions are not arbitrary. They have a technical dimension relating to the demands of the material: the vase has to hold water, the song has to be in the singer's range. But these demands also have an expressive dimension; decisions are made because they help shape the work according to its aptness for what the work is saying.

Those creative decisions are enshrined in the formal properties of the work. Most composers experience the act of composition as a balance of their own creative will and the demands of their material, a force that seems to make demands of the composer rather than vice versa. And the force of the work, the way its energy is structured, is met by the performer and the listener; it is this to which we attend, not to the composer. To do this, we must be fluent in musical codes just as we must be fluent in both literary codes and language to understand novels and poems. The problems facing classical music hinge on the fact that we no longer share the musical codes that would make it meaningful. For many people, classical music is no more significant than that snippet of foreign language caught on the radio: it means "classical" the way a few foreign words mean "Germanness." Of course it has a host of other connotations—of class, tradition, history, education, wealth, and so on—but in much the same way that "Germanness" has a host of connotations for an Englishman who doesn't speak German.

Perhaps this is overstated. After all, as I've commented earlier, classical music is all around us: on TV, in films, in shopping centers, stations, restaurants, and phone systems. Its use in film and on TV is particularly important because there it contributes to a significant experience even for people who may not normally listen to it. Perhaps, then, there is a level at which classical music is better understood by a general audience than we might imagine. Most people today encounter the classical repertoire through film and TV music. It is doubtful, however, that this enhances an understanding of classical music. Film music, where it relates to classical music at all, is derived from the style of earlier ages. Indeed, it is a strange historical anomaly that contemporary film music employs musical clichés deriving from a hundred years or so earlier, not as pastiche for historical dramas but as the principal materials for contemporary scores. While this may work well for films, it has a particular effect on the experience of a generation whose principal enculturation in classical music has been through film music. Not only does film music employ nineteenth-century musical materials; it does so as self-contained narrative signs rather than part of an autonomous musical discourse, which is how these materials functioned in the nineteenth-century symphonic tradition. The consequences are clear: the contemporary audience tends to deal with classical materials only in an atomistic way and only inasmuch as they denote some narrative or visual "meaning." Schooled on Hollywood film scores, one can recognize the musical materials in Tchaikovsky, Rachmaninoff, Mahler, Strauss —even Debussy, Stravinsky, and Schoenberg—but be unable to follow the discourse that arises from these materials. And failure to follow the discourse means a failure to grasp the significance of materials in their original discursive context. A generation brought up on film music is apt to dismiss Mahler's music, for example, as sentimental or histrionic because some of the key moments of his symphonic discourses employ materials that have become so in the context of film music. Yet Mahler's symphonies are *not* sentimental in the way that the derived film score may be, because sentimentality is not solely defined by the materials; it is defined by the authenticity with which those materials are arrived at, their coherence within the whole.

Meaning is neither arbitrary nor absolute. Culture is defined by this tension between our subjective freedom to interpret things and their social objectivity. Poetry is founded on such a freedom—on the tension between the social objectivity of a shared language and the imaginative spaces opened up by our creative (mis)readings. To forget this is to separate the poles between which the tension of meaning is generated and to dissolve culture into an endless and formless world of private, schizophrenic meanings; it is to abolish the possibility of meaning. Not only are meanings not arbitrary in relation to their objects, neither are they equally valid. My eight-year-old son has the ability to read Kant (in a literal sense) just as he has the ability to listen to Beethoven. But my understanding of Kant and Beethoven is greater than his. This simple fact tends to be obscured by a cultural studies approach that, in its theoretical inflation of the different meanings attributed to Kant and Beethoven by my son and me, implies that our interpretations are equally valid points on a flat cultural map.

In approaching a musical text objectively, the point is not to elucidate some hackneyed "hidden meaning" (as generations of schoolchildren imagined the study of poetry was for). Nor does it have to do with knowing the composer's intentions, reading the program note, or performing complex analysis. It has nothing to do with interpretation in terms of seeking to *explain* the music in extramusical terms. It remains centrally connected to the idea of our experience but is distinct from our immediate or appetitive enjoyment of the work. Music, as has often been said, is meaningful without having a paraphrasable meaning, is expressive without necessarily communicating something denoted by any linguistic expression. A far more useful term than "meaning," "expression," or "interpretation" is that of "understanding." The goal of our relationship with music-as-art, I suggest, is understanding.

Understanding what? Simply understanding, as an intransitive activity. We come into empathy with another. We share the journey in which artworks invite us to participate, and we understand. The inadequacy of linguistic formulas for its expression is by no means a demonstration of the absence of content. Leaving the concert hall after a performance of Mahler's Ninth Symphony, one is unlikely to say that the music is without content. One may be inwardly shattered, having understood the music very well and precisely for that reason refusing the clichés by which program-note writers struggle to articulate its link to a verbal discourse.

ELITISM

I am not concerned with the history of the term "elitism," with what it should mean in a strict sense nor any other philosophical niceties about what is and isn't elitist. My initial concern is how the term is most frequently employed with reference to classical music and to art and high culture more generally. Few other words have so single-handedly prevented rational thinking and debate about the issues surrounding art and society, and few terms can match its damning force. It ends the argument about art before it has even started: if art is elitist, it seems, no more need be said about it. Whatever else art may be, if it is elitist, it is indefensible. The term is applied to certain kinds of art and to the people who participate in that art. The two are, of course, quite separate issues, but the use of the same word for both implies an overriding connection: this art is elitist because it is the art of elitist people; those who associate themselves with elitist art must themselves be elitist.

Applied to people, it is a damning term. To be elitist implies that one is not only snobbish and pretentious but also out of touch with contemporary culture, with its disregard for old divisions of high and low, art and entertainment. Worse, it suggests a serious political incorrectness: in offending against the pseudo-democracy of culture, it implies that one is politically undemocratic in a literal sense. Because one does not believe in the equal validity of all cultural products, it is assumed that one is somehow opposed to the equal rights of people. Elitist people have the privilege (literally, "private law") that comes with wealth, social status, and education.

People are accused of cultural elitism because they participate in activities perceived as being closed to others (because of economic and class barriers). And so long as these activities are primarily perceived by their outward signs (dress codes and rich living, in particular), the perception will validate itself.

More offensive than the economic wealth associated with high culture is the larger social privilege for which it seems to stand. Involvement in high art often does originate in educational privilege, whether or not accompanied by economic privilege. And perhaps even more damning is that an interest in high culture seems to claim a higher ground, an involvement in higher things built on a more refined taste. It is, so the usual criticism runs, above all, pretentious. Not only do those involved in high culture have pretensions above themselves; they also seek to defend that space by discourses designed to alienate others and deny them access. Central to these is the discourse of art itself, and most of all modern art, which is forever trying to be clever, avoiding simple communication, and valuing artists whose work confounds the general public. Indeed, many might think that, in modern art, the more esoteric the artists, the more they seem to be valued.

That art has often been used, and continues to be used, as a sign of social elitism is not hard to demonstrate. But far more serious is the charge that art or music is *itself* elitist. I have argued that the musical object should be considered apart from the conditions of its social use as an irreducible element of its social meaning. So the notion that music itself might be elitist thus needs to be taken seriously. "Difficult" modernist music is especially likely to be dismissed as elitist on the grounds that the language it employs appears to be meaningful to only a tiny group of intellectuals, theorists, and composers. It fails to appeal immediately, even to a broad base of classical "music lovers," and is thus exclusive in a way that music should not be. Good music, runs this argument, appeals directly to a broad range of people (and "great" music to virtually everyone). Why else should composers deliberately write such esoteric and generally repellent music except to construct some hyperexclusive cultural capital?

This perception of willful exclusion adds vehemence to the charge of elitism—coupled with a resistance to the idea of culture being judged and graded at all. Art and music that are labeled elitist could just as well be called minority (an elite is by definition a minority) except for this perception of opposition, of high versus low. If classical music were only something minority, akin to a sport like polo, it might be less offensive. It might then be perceived as an essentially harmless activity pursued by a privileged minority, certainly exclusive but peripheral to most people's concerns. But people who play polo tend to keep quiet about it and let the majority enjoy other sports like football or cricket; they don't speak out in the media or write books about the superiority of polo over other sports, argue that it deserves a special place in educational curricula, or demand public subsidies to fund the already privileged minority that enjoys it.

The work of educationalists and bodies like the Arts Council or the NEA is designed to make the high arts more accessible, suggesting that the charge of elitism as willful exclusion is unfounded. But the charge sticks nevertheless because of the apparent high-handedness with which certain kinds of art and music are judged to be important for us all (if only we had sufficient physical and educational access to them). For all its democratic rhetoric, this movement does not relinquish the basic tenet that some art-works are more valuable than others and, more precisely, that high art has a value not conferred upon popular culture. Great art may become more accessible (through cheaper tickets, educational outreach programs, and opera on TV), but this comes with a quiet insistence that one should knuckle down and work at it until it becomes enjoyable, because it's good for you in a way that the immediate pleasures of popular culture are not.

Recently this rather paternalistic, pedagogical tone has changed. The at-tempts of the BBC and other institutions to insist that the audience should measure up to the challenge of difficult music have largely been displaced by a marketing approach for classical music—especially contemporary music—that begins with the potential audience rather than the music. The *New Audiences* program sponsored in the United Kingdom by the Depart-ment for Culture, Media, and Sport is less about getting new audiences to listen to music they've been uninterested in for the last thirty years and more about programming a different kind of music. The attempt to popu-larize classical music, let alone contemporary classical music, is under-mined by the fact that music-as-art refuses to be appropriated solely in terms of the immediacy demanded by popular culture. If this makes the music elitist (and for many people it does), then it is elitist in the same way and to the same degree that philosophy or mathematics is elitist, that learning a foreign language is elitist, that astronomy, nuclear physics, and space exploration is elitist. It is a historical peculiarity of contemporary so-ciety that we seem to think of music exclusively as the source of immedi-ate pleasure, akin to our attitude toward food or clothes or sex, rather than as one of the most sophisticated forms of human discourse by which we represent and negotiate our understanding of ourselves and the world. To be sure, these contradictory claims and uses have always existed in musical practice; they go to the heart of music's contradictory nature as something both immediately pleasurable and also exceeding the immediate. What is worrisome about contemporary musical practice is the loss of tension between these elements and the reduction of music to a much smaller function. Only recently have we collectively reduced music to the question of immediate pleasure alone, such that choosing between different musical types is no more significant than choosing between different flavors of ice cream. This is the fundamental difference between the claim of music as art and the claim of music as entertainment.

I find it hard to imagine that we would accuse science of being elitist, and yet it, too, requires learning and has its experts, its privileging of resources for the few who participate in it, its jargon, and so on. We celebrate this because we still have faith that it delivers things of practical value to us all (although much pure science does no such thing, of course). But science is bolstered by a legitimating discourse that is not seriously threatened even by its periodic questioning (over issues such as nuclear power, genetically modified foods, or embryo research). Until relatively recently, art has been supported by a similar kind of legitimation: even when it seemed to involve a minority, what it accomplished was of benefit (however unseen) to the whole community. That legitimation is now all but gone, ironically at the same time that art as commodity and artifact has become more accessible than ever.

It is by no means coincidental, of course, that (in Walter Benjamin's terms) art loses its magical aura in the age of its mechanical reproduction. Because art becomes part of the everyday, it ceases to function as something extraordinary. This is the price of a democratization of art resulting from reproductive technologies that make art more available than ever before. The magical aura with which original paintings and artifacts are still surrounded has been proven false—as an ideological claim to be something other than a man-made object—but it points to a significant loss. One subscribed to this illusory auratic quality of art because it served as a symbol for our belief that objects, including ourselves and the world, might also be sacred, that they might be more than the sum of their parts. The loss of art's aura is thus more than a demystification, a deconstruction of art's magical properties; it is also coterminous with the triumph of a materialism that reduces the world and ourselves to the status of things. This is why the power of an art form like classical music is neutralized in today's culture: it ceases to work when it is treated as simply a thing among others, a thing to be used by and for the subject. Art proposes itself as a special kind of object that, through its internal organization, transcends its thinglike quality by being taken up as thought, as an intellectual or spiritual activity rather than merely a physical, perceptual, or sensuous one.

Art claims to fulfill what religious icons and the doctrine of transubstantiation once claimed: that a material object becomes more than the sum of its material parts, that it projects a spiritual energy. In this way, high art realizes, in secular form, what was once the domain of religion. And as with religious icons, what begins as authentic experience may deteriorate into fetishism and outward observance. The object does not literally possess a magical power, but it invites a kind of participation from the subject that results in "miraculous" things. In a religious context, this was a matter of faith, of ritual and collective belief. Art, too demands a certain kind of attention, but it is far more shaped by the form of the object and the experience it facilitates. It does not necessarily deliver an experience most people would call religious, but art, even when it is most obviously concerned with the secular, implies something beyond itself, and in this sense it is metaphysical.

The irony that art's metaphysical yearning should be reduced to a material function (distinguishing class position) in an age when great art is more accessible than ever before is only one of several ironies arising from the contemporary dismissal of classical music as elitist. Not the least of these is the fact that the original popularity of classical music derived from its democratic appeal, the aspiration of inclusiveness expressed in its fusion of high and low. But a particularly acute irony is that the society that labels classical music elitist also ensures that it continues to be so. Willful exclusion aside, what prevents people from participating in music-as-art comes down to problems of literacy—or "style competence," as it is sometimes more euphemistically called. This is a far more profound barrier to understanding music than ticket prices or the perceived class structure of the audience; without it, classical music is, for all intents and purposes, inaccessible. What has previously been denied because of genuine class privilege is now denied because of the cultural associations of that earlier class distinction. In this way, the relative sidelining of classical music, even by the middle classes, arises in part from a collective desire to distance oneself from these associations of earlier privilege. This dismissal is as fickle as it is superficial, as demonstrated by the fact that more recently a new middle-class market for classical music has grown (in tandem with its role in advertising) precisely because of those earlier associations of wealth and social status.

There is thus a danger that those who embrace classical music, no less than those who dismiss it, ensure that it will remain a sign of social separation. Just as a certain audience is happy to keep high culture as its own preserve, entrenched resentment at the inaccessibility of high culture leads to policies that ensure its continued inaccessibility. On the whole, classical music is marginalized by the mass media, which reciprocally confirm and reproduce the general perception that it is too difficult, too heavy, and too low in immediate pleasure content. But the same mass media readily frame complaints about the privilege of high art, a privilege that need not exist anymore but that is sustained, in part, by its systematic marginalization in the mass media. This situation, comprehensible within the logic of commercial organizations, is hard to defend in educational contexts. By failing to provide instrumental tuition, schools ensure that only children from relatively well-off families will learn an instrument. They thus reproduce and reinforce a class privilege that free schooling was meant to alleviate. Children leaving school at age sixteen or eighteen without the cultural tools (including self-confidence) to engage with so-called high culture have not been well served by their education—an education that has avoided high culture on the grounds that it is elitist, thus reproducing the division it professes to oppose.

Elitism as willful, snobbish exclusivity stinks. It should be opposed and shown up for what it is. But "elitism" is an inflammatory word, one that licenses anything carried out under its banner and thus becomes a dangerous form of political correctness. One version equates with the attempt to expunge Culture from culture—that is, to rid everyday life of the irritant of art. Insisting that there is no place for something to which not everyone has immediate access is the social revenge against the assumptions of an earlier age that only Culture (high art) mattered and culture (everyday life) was of no concern. But nobody wins in exacting this kind of historical class revenge. If a beautiful sandy cove in Cornwall had been reserved for two hundred years for the private use of a single family, do we now maliciously bury it in concrete or work toward making it accessible to the public? High art and classical music *used* to be the preserve of an elite; whether it remains so is up to us.

No amount of marketing strategies, outreach programs, and grants for "new audiences" can get around the fact that art is sometimes difficult stuff. While art can make a broad, immediate, and often intense appeal, it can also require time, care, and a nonappetitive approach that most people associate with study or work. But the outer limits of human invention are hardly to be understood in a lunch hour or as an accompaniment to negotiating rush-hour traffic. Those who reject what cannot be immediately grasped as obscure and thus elitist have a strange sense of democracy and undervalue both the reach and aspiration of the human spirit. Five hundred years ago, political democracy was thought to be impossible because the broad mass of the population was illiterate. How politically correct would it look now to have dug in one's heels with the argument that "reading is elitist and imposes the interests of a dominant class on a working poor who have no interest in books"?

The charge of artistic elitism is sometimes the denial not only of things that are the source of potential pleasure and enjoyment to a wider audience, but also of things that are concerned with essential aspects of humanity. The lack of any real cultural critique allows us to accept murky uses of words like "elitism" without scrutinizing them more carefully. Saying so is the height of political incorrectness, and I am fully aware that some readers will already be closed to any rational argument about this topic because of the deafening buzz generated by the word. A sign of how bad this situation has become is the fact that the academy itself, whose only real justification is as a protected game reserve for rigorous thinking and the critical distance it delivers, now panders to general naïveté on these issues. Academics undermine their own purpose when they allow guilt about their own education and a sense of social uselessness to tempt them into swapping intellectual distance for "social relevance" and political correctness. Real intellectual work is increasingly eclipsed by comment, opinion, and journalese—endlessly ironic, friends with everybody and nobody, believing ultimately in nothing. We live in a digest culture in which an unwillingness to engage in sustained thought rapidly becomes a hostility toward it. Before long, the hostility masks an incapacity to do so. This is glaringly obvious in the case of music, debate about which is skewed by the partial truth that it engages its listeners directly and immediately. The ideology of pure immediacy in music is almost as hostile toward thought *about* music as toward thought *in* music. The meager legacy of an autonomous subject is the defense of the right to ignorance, an assertion of the right to utterly subjective judgment. Our culture is not just ignorant; it is stubbornly and arrogantly so.

There are two separate, hopelessly entwined issues in the concept of elitism. One originates in genuine social inequalities, the other in a definitive human aspiration to exceed the limits of oneself and one's immediate surroundings. The undermining of one by the other might be summed up in the idea of being pretentious. Not only are artworks dismissed as pretentious; so are those who engage in them. Art *is* pretense: it is artifice, something made, not something natural. It *can* be used as a denial of life, a turning away into artificial worlds that pretend to be something they are not. Art can be pretentious, and it can be used pretentiously. But perhaps the term implies, however negatively, a certain authenticity. The critical edge in dismissing something or somebody as pretentious expresses a deep-seated disappointment that what is promised turns out to be false; bitterness toward art expresses a certain disappointment that things are not as art suggests they might be. There is a flip side to the perceived elitism of art: its "pretentious" difficulties arise as a result of its striving to exceed the everyday. The human spirit aspires to be more than one is, to have a greater, richer experience of the world, to transcend the limits of one's immediate surroundings and experience of the world and of oneself. That, in short, is what art is about. Few people live like that all the time, and perhaps it is the implication that one should that is most resented. Most of us need what popular culture does, too, which primarily has to do with mediating our present. Art is fundamentally utopian: it embodies the human hope that the world and we who inhabit it might be remade. As such, it is critical of the here and now even as it redeems it.

CHAPTER 5. THE OLD, THE NEW, AND THE CONTEMPORARY

Classical music is generally considered old music. This is important both for those who value it highly and for those who consider it largely irrelevant today. A common argument for the first position is that this music has stood the test of time and been judged as "great music" by successive generations. It survives, so runs this argument, because it has a universal and timeless quality that transcends the fluctuations of cultural fashion. The opposing position argues that classical music is the product of an earlier century and speaks primarily to and about that time. It has little or no relevance to a modern age to which it cannot speak.

Neither position is adequately argued, but the age of classical music remains significant. For many, classical music is rather like the traditional oil paintings that hang in large public galleries. Both the gallery and the concert hall often seem similar in atmosphere to the museum. All three can be reminiscent of the church in that they command a certain aura of the sacred long after the things they contain have ceased to be part of people's daily lives. The respect that they retain arises from a mixture of awe at the archaic and monumental and a culturally learned reverence for certain objects and practices. But even the well-disposed can find this atmosphere rather stifling, and sometimes we leave these buildings with a sense of release, like swimmers coming up for air. The longevity of classical music is certainly a factor in the rather grudging general respect it still commands, but like the artifacts in a museum, it can appear very distant from the realities of daily life. On the other hand, this distance is undoubtedly part of the appeal for those who use classical music as an outward sign of their own "classical" taste. With its origins in an essentially aristocratic society, classical music continues to serve, all too often, as an indicator of social class or status.

These origins in an earlier stage of European society have been the subject of recent academic scrutiny. The main thrust has been to show as false the claim that classical music is autonomous—in other words, to demonstrate that it does not exist in a closed, ideal space of its own, unaffected by the real world. Such scholarship reveals how this music is connected to the world in which it is made and used, and shows how it is bound up with real social conditions. For some, this rather iconoclastic turn in musicology suggests a devaluing of classical music. Beethoven's music was once understood in terms of Enlightenment ideals of freedom and universal community, but now it appears to be riven with the dominating structures of the composer's patriarchal society and a repressive male sexuality. Music, by this model, reproduces the ideologies of its age, and the nineteenth century seems to be an age from which we are particularly keen to distance ourselves. Our modernity, we imagine, separates us from the world of the nineteenth century, which we happily dismiss as authoritarian, elitist, and politically suspect—a century of capitalism, imperialism, and patriarchalism. Listening to Beethoven, so runs this argument, necessarily involves one in colluding with the ideologies of his age.

The superficiality of this argument is not hard to demonstrate. It is based on a peculiar characteristic of the postmodern age—the radical shrinking of our notion of the present. Theories of modernity disagree about the starting point of our modern world, with the start of the twentieth century, the eighteenth-century Enlightenment, and the Renaissance all being possible contenders. All are at odds with a dominant consciousness that assumes the modern is confined to the past few years, confusing modernity (which is defined in part by a set of ideas) with what is recent (which is merely chronological). Perhaps this contraction of the present is a feature of technological modernity—the greater the pace of change, the shorter our sense of the present. This logic is certainly replicated in the dynamic of much popular music, whose rapid turnover of styles is in part related to the rapid changes in the technology central to its production. Classical music, on the other hand, is often distinguished by its apparent lack of connection with technological innovation. It seems stubbornly content with acoustic instruments that predate the discovery of electricity. For some, this makes it hopelessly outdated and irrelevant; for others, it undoubtedly adds to classical music's subliminal appeal as a sign of a preindustrial arcadia. Of course, since most people now encounter classical music primarily in recorded form, its presence is thoroughly mediated by contemporary audio technology.

It should be remembered that a reverence for cultural history is itself a cultural idea of relatively recent invention. Significantly, our concern with music of the past is largely a product of the rise of classical music. An interest in older music, such as the work of Palestrina, Bach, and Handel, arose as composers became self-conscious about their historical status and, with Beethoven in particular, developed the idea of composing not just for the present but for some notion of posterity, for those who follow. Before that, almost all music was by definition contemporary music. This was, more generally, a time in which our modern historical consciousness was formed, bound up with the notions of historical progression that remain a defining part of the modern world. This period also saw the high claims made for art and music that still inform our thinking. The category of history is therefore an essential part of the modern and thus of modern ideals such as democracy and self-determination.

A more problematic question is posed by "new" classical music, an awkward phrase that underlines the awkwardness of our historical understanding. If new classical music meant pastiche Mozart, we could catalog classical music and its pre-electric instruments as a closed body of material derived from an earlier age. But new classical music (or contemporary music, as it prefers to be called) strikes most people as fiercely modern, so much so that modern music (as its detractors prefer to call it) seems to embody the most negative aspects of modern life—dissonance, alienation, anxiety, and meaninglessness. This paradox causes problems for both the lover of older classical music and the listener who cares for no classical music at all. It claims a relation to the past that works both ways: something two hundred years old is related to the modern, and a contemporary work is shaped by the past. It forces us to acknowledge that we are bound up with our history and suggests that a modern culture wrestles with this acknowledgment, with trying to distinguish itself as new in relation to the old. Perhaps it is no exaggeration to suggest that the denial of the claims of classical music is a sign of a more general contemporary denial of the historical and a stubborn insistence on the one-dimensional surface of the present.

In other words, Beethoven may yet be relevant to the modern age because our age is bound up with his. In particular, some of our most central concepts (of society as of art) derive from the period in which he was working: ideas of the autonomous individual subject, authentic self-expression, a society of free individuals, and a reconciliation of nature with human society. Beethoven's age, like our own, wrestled with these ideas despite society's tendency toward their opposites; this is precisely why his music might still be of interest to us. No art worth the name is simply the reproduction of dominant ideologies. No art worth the name is entirely "politically correct." Art reworks and reformulates its social materials, and while it may reinforce dominant ideologies, it may also undermine them and critically reconfigure their terms. No art escapes the discursive tension between its presentation of elements of the existing order and the image of the new arising from their reformulation.

For all that, there is a distinctly uncomfortable, even embattled feeling among those who defend classical music as part of the educational curriculum or as a recipient of state subsidy. The opposition seems to have the upper hand with their suggestion that classical music is tainted with the sins of its own age—the product of "dead white males" with little relevance for today's multicultural world. But this blank dismissal underestimates the extent to which artworks define their critical space, and it denies that they are often made in spite of their own age or even deliberately against it, rather than merely reflecting it. The age of Mozart and Haydn, or even Mahler and Debussy, may seem distant to us, but the questions of human identity and self-understanding that such music confronts are also our own. They are not, to be sure, obviously concerned with race, class, or gender. From this, one might conclude that classical music is ideological, guilty of covering up the material tensions of social life. But one might also conclude that this music deals instead with those aspects of human life that still remain to be confronted when the battles of race, class, and gender are won, or simply those inner moments of anxiety, emptiness, or sheer wonder that are not addressed by the merely political.

For this reason, classical music retains the capacity to shed the social baggage that has often weighed it down. Rather than drowning under that weight, it might float back to the surface, reappearing to make forceful contemporary claims. It is, perhaps, no more than a matter of our personal and collective choices. The difficulty is that, because classical music is rarely presented from this perspective, one of its most distinctive claims and part of its unique value have been lost to debate. The real significance of the historical in classical music lies in its *proximity* to our age. But the historical aspect is used for quite opposite purposes both by those selling classical music (who make it exotic in that way) and by those undermining its claims to a special status (who make it irrelevant in that way). Paradoxically, then, the historical distance of classical music from our age is exaggerated by those who defend its contemporary value just as much as by those who dismiss it. One fetishizes the past (presented as a self-contained, idyllic state), and the other fetishizes the present (experienced solely through the thin timescales of personal rather than historical perspectives). Contemporary culture undoubtedly favors the latter, whose concern with the new seems allied to a progressive claim, whereas valuing the old for its own sake is easily allied to a conservative and even regressive position.

Art, however, makes a radical claim about the passage of time and the wearing out of things. It is at odds with the logic of a consumer society that sees the old as somehow "used up" and therefore to be discarded. It opposes the logic of a technocratic society that judges the old as necessarily more rudimentary and primitive and thus superseded by the new. In a word, art is antithetical to fashion and a culture fundamentally directed by fashion. Artworks persist within this climate, but whether or not they continue to function *as art* is a rather different matter. Where they do, it is because the cliché that art is timeless is not without its grain of truth. Artworks are most certainly of their time: everything from their physical materials to their ideas and constitutive formal tensions speak of the world in which they were made. But they also project a content that self-evidently slices through time, transcends its power over the material, and strikes us with a force that vivifies our present experience with a unique intensity. In doing so, art exerts a powerful symbolic force: it redeems what is past by bringing it into a living relationship with the present. This redemptive function contradicts a one-dimensional view of time in which what is past is immediately lost. That old artworks can resonate within us, with a force greater than much of what constitutes "the present," suggests an aspect of our being that is similarly untrammeled by time. In a profound sense, this is why art claims a spiritual function, one that has nothing to do with the materialism of fashion. Fashion shrinks from the past and clings anxiously to the immediacy of the present. In doing so, it condemns us all, since we, too, inevitably become the past. The intensity with which we consume the newness of things is ultimately a symptom of our fear of death. And the vicious circle of a culture dominated by this logic is such that the tighter we cling to the mere novelty of things, the greater our refusal of those elements that cut across time. Cultural obsession with the new simply reflects an impossible flight from death.

Art has not been well served by an older approach that treated it as "unworldly" and placed it on a pedestal in the museum, or by a more recent approach that emphasizes its thoroughly historical and worldly aspect. Taken separately, both are inadequate and fail to grasp a definitive quality of art—that it is both of these things at once. The pedestal approach has undoubtedly turned many people off; classical music has often been surrounded by unnecessary formality and an academic pedantry that is apt to strike noninitiates as hollow elitism. More than that, the implication that classical music is removed from the everyday neutralizes part of its essential force. But Puccini's *La Bohème* is about students who fall in love, the brevity of youth, and, by implication, our regret that such intensity of experience is ephemeral. Mozart's *Marriage of Figaro* is a comedy of sexual and class power relations in which the "ordinary" people get the better of their social masters, but in which ultimately the vulnerability and humanity of all are celebrated. These are big, timeless themes, but they are treated through individual characters whose lives connect with our own— if no longer outwardly, then certainly inwardly. We would do better to accentuate Mozart's proximity to us, not his distance. The museum culture that surrounds his music, all powdered wigs and frock coats, is not helpful. But when, in *Figaro*, the countess sings of the poignancy of a relationship that has become moribund compared to the vitality of the young love she sees around her, doesn't she touch on an aspect of human relationships that transcends, in the opening line of her aria, the two centuries between Mozart's age and our own?

TRUTH, LIES, AND MUSICAL NONSENSE

Music's capacity to move us in these ways is often seen as mysterious and inexplicable. Whereas we all have some experience of writing, for most of us composing music remains a closed book. More so than in the other arts, the origins of a musical work are explained almost exclusively through vague ideas of inspiration and genius. But all composers know that a musical work is something made, often painstakingly, from the recalcitrant materials that form its initial ideas. To say that musical composition is an act of construction is not to deny categories of creativity or inspiration, but to insist that the musical piece is literally a "work," a labor exerted upon the building blocks of musical language.

Perhaps the resistance to seeing music as something constructed, rather than something born of inspirational rapture, works against the idea that music might be made badly. It is not that we don't make judgments about music, but these hinge almost entirely on our own pleasure rather than how the piece is made. Elsewhere in daily life, we feel more confident about judging objectively whether a thing is well-made or not. We return goods that are faulty and send back a meal that is undercooked. We can make judgments about performers because their function is reasonably well defined. That I am not as good a pianist as Alfred Brendel is a statement with which none of my students would disagree. In sport, judgments of quality are built into the game. The best sprinter is the one who covers the distance in the fastest time. There are no points for style, dress sense, or crowd-pleasing.

With artworks it is rather more difficult, because here the task to be accomplished is less clearly defined, yet this culture of ranking art has become increasingly pervasive. Awards in both the pop and classical music industries rest on the claim that one can make a judgment about the quality of musical works as well as performers, just as Oscars and Baftas imply as much about films and those who make them. In some cases, the judgment is made by a panel of experts, but often it is the result of a popular vote. Here the winner should, of course, more properly carry the accolade "most popular" rather than "best," but this difference becomes so blurred in the entertainment industry that the terms are synonymous. The purpose of an athlete is thus to run fast or jump high, and the purpose of an entertainer is to be popular. Both judgments are legitimated by the fact that they are made on a strictly quantitative basis.

But by what criteria can we assess the quality of an artwork that does not claim entertainment as its primary function and for which popularity may therefore be inadequate as a yardstick? Let's go back to the point that music is something made; it is composed or written in ways analogous to the ways novels, plays, or film scripts are written. With the writing of words we are on more familiar ground, since we all have some experience of writing, even if only at school. What does it mean when a teacher corrects a student's written work? The teacher's comments are, to a large extent, not a matter of personal taste but claim a level of objectivity. We look to teachers to assess writing critically, to point out basic errors in grammar and spelling as well as more involved weaknesses such as a tendency to repetition and an unordered or unconnected series of statements. A good teacher recognizes the difference between an unimaginative reproduction of familiar ideas and original and independent work. The grades a teacher awards, on the basis of such criteria, are not arbitrary but are likely to be broadly in line with the independent assessments of other teachers. There is, then, a communal agreement about the difference between bad and good writing, an agreement that carries objective weight.

Music is not literally a language, but it displays qualities that make it, in some respects, analogous to language. The music teacher can correct musical writing in much the same way that the English teacher can correct essay writing. Musicians know the difference between what works and what doesn't and have a highly developed, self-critical awareness of how well something is played or made. For a musician, listening to badly written music is like taking part in an inane or even nonsensical conversation. Teachers know the disorientation and frustration that sets in when reading an essay with badly constructed sentences and poorly presented ideas; exactly the same can apply to musical composition where musical ideas are insufficiently differentiated. Pieces of music can be like bad essays—bland, overly repetitive, and unoriginal. This is a question not of subjective response but rather of the objective construction of the piece, of the materials it uses and the way it organizes them.

One of the distinguishing features of the music we label "classical" is that it is, to a high degree, self-reflective about its own language. The history of that music reveals a constant tension between its inward, linguistic concerns and an outward concern to speak to its audience. These demands are not necessarily in harmony. Philosophical prose may be excellently written and exhibit a rare degree of intellectual rigor yet be nearly unreadable by the nonphilosopher. The same is true of a complex mathematical equation for the nonmathematician. Music can behave in the same way (and at times it has), but on the whole it successfully balances this linguistic, constructional aspect with an immediacy that defines music as art and distinguishes it from philosophy or mathematics. Composers achieve that balance in many ways, resulting in larger or smaller differences in musical style. Some composers, caught up in the demands of the linguistic aspect of their art, have neglected the needs of a nonspecialist audience for an immediacy of musical surface. Bach's *Goldberg Variations*, Beethoven's late quartets, and Webern's serial works might all serve as examples. Others have taken far more care of their audience's demands at the expense of the inner consistency or richness of development of their musical materials. Some of Vivaldi's concertos, Hummel's piano sonatas, and Copland's orchestral music might serve as examples. Every composer has to balance this equation, and every age shows composers making different emphases. Composers have also made conscious decisions to change the emphasis for certain works: C. P. E. Bach, for example, distinguished between sets of keyboard sonatas with the labels "for connoisseurs and amateurs," "easy sonatas," and even "sonatas for ladies."

Much of the difficulty attributed to classical music derives from a concern with its linguistic character. To take this music on its own terms means engaging with its linguistic, propositional, and thus intellectual element. From this perspective, the popularity of a piece is no guarantee of its quality. Indeed, it is entirely possible that music approached for the immediacy of its surface may be linguistically weak or even inane. While dazzling the ear with attractive sounds, the piece may still get no further linguistically than the equivalent of repeating the undeveloped propositions children meet in their first reading books: "John likes the dog," "Janet likes the dog." Of course, if we don't listen linguistically we may not notice this discrepancy. Where music works as background music, as long as its immediate surface is attractive, it can be grammatical nonsense and not disturb us. If we want music simply to surround us with a certain sound-world, we may not notice or care about its lack of genuinely thoughtful activity.

The degree to which music is intellectually coherent is not an abstract question, comparable to a mathematical equation; it is a historical one. Musical materials and their meanings change over time. When Stravinsky used a C major chord in 1930 it had a different meaning than the same C major chord Bach used in 1730. It may be identical acoustically, but its musical resonance in two historical and cultural contexts is quite different. One might find parallels in how words change their meaning across centuries or how dress codes alter. What was daring, modern, and exclusive two hundred years ago may today make a classical, conservative, and rather clichéd statement. In the same way, the choices composers make about their musical materials and techniques are shaped by their historical location. Moreover, the language of Western art music exhibits a degree of historical change that far exceeds that of modern spoken languages like English, French, or German. The musical language of Mozart is different to that of Bach writing fifty years earlier, just as it is different from that of Berlioz writing fifty years later. Composers' voices are both personal (Mozart sounds different from Haydn) and thoroughly mediated by their historical and cultural location (Mozart and Haydn share a common musical legacy of late-eighteenth-century Viennese society). The personal aspect arises not from some essential stylistic pattern that could turn up just as easily in another age, but rather from choices, emphases, and deviations made *within* the historically available language.

Just as I have only the vocabulary and grammatical structures of English available to me as I write, so every composer works within a bounded field of musical language. What makes music different is its capacity to reformulate its language and to use elements in ways that might at first seem perplexing, but this play with conventions presumes the existence of those conventions in the first place. Composers work at their ideas; they make corrections and deletions, reject certain options in favor of others, develop their ideas in one way rather than another. They make judgments that one thing is more satisfying, meaningful, or effective than another. That they do so presumes that they recognize options that do not work—that are less satisfying, meaningful, or effective.

Since at least the mid–eighteenth century and the origins of classical music, composers have worked in a context that was increasingly historically self-conscious. Certain materials or techniques were no longer thinkable in the musical work because they had become archaic and thus seemed "untrue" as materials for a contemporary work. To simply reproduce archaic materials, uncritically and without reformulation, would be to deny the individuality and originality that the musical artwork came to symbolize from the late eighteenth century onward. Not to reformulate materials in some way, to be unoriginal, would be to deny the essential idea of the age: the creative originality of the individual. Music's "truth" was thus linked to its capacity for enacting within its formal processes the self-development of the autonomous subject. To be unoriginal was thus to be false, to speak with others' words and others' thoughts—to be inauthentic.

No significant composer of art music has ever written in a manner that was completely unaware of what has already taken place in music. There are no significant nineteenth-century composers writing music in a thoroughly baroque idiom, as if they were still in the seventeenth century. And until at least the end of the nineteenth century, there was a generally shared understanding of developments in musical language across genres and national contexts. Puccini, writing in 1900, showed plenty of awareness of Strauss and Debussy even though his music remains distinct from theirs. Mahler, writing at the same time, may have written only symphonies and songs, but his music is imbued with the developments Wagner made in the operatic genre. After 1900, the picture becomes much more complex. Not only does modernism in music, as in visual art or literature, result in the fragmentation of a shared language into many styles, but there is also a much greater distance between "centers" of modernist innovation and "peripheries" in which musical language changed less radically. Thus, before World War II, the atonal revolution of the Second Viennese School (Schoenberg, Berg, and Webern) finds little echo outside of Austria. One need only mention the names of other contemporaneous composers to make the point that regionalism and other aesthetic perspectives were equally potent forces: consider the music of Poulenc, Sibelius, Vaughan Williams, Janáček, Rachmaninoff, and Copland. But this fragmentation within modernism itself was further complicated by a bifurcation between art music and popular culture that is itself a symptom of modernism.

Until the beginning of the twentieth century, so-called high and low culture coexisted in symbiotic fashion. Their greater separation after 1900 is a result of modernism's deliberate refusal of an increasingly dominant entertainment function. Modernism is bound up with artists who reaffirmed the high spiritual and intellectual function of art that the early romantics had claimed a century earlier, but that even then was in tension with a tendency for its expanding audience to treat it as entertainment. It is thus a definitive tension of classical music, there from the start and still with us today. This tension is exhibited in music's outward function, but it is also related to differing attitudes toward music's internal construction—its use of particular musical materials and techniques. Art music has increasingly separated itself from more popular forms by emphasizing a developing musical language whose historical transformations constitute an essential element of the style.

From the perspective of classical music, therefore, a pop ballad of the 1950s is perplexing not so much because of the simplicity of the musical materials, which might be compared in some respects to the simplicity of Schubert, but precisely because the ballad was written in the 1950s and not the 1820s. For all the superficial modernity of the sound-world, the song's harmonic and melodic materials and the naive simplicity of its form seem to deny the changes in musical language of the intervening 130 years. From a musical point of view, this is as odd as denying 130 years of history. It would be as unthinkable as adopting other aspects of 1820s culture, such as its dress codes, ways of speaking, or available technology.

In those 130 years, musical language has changed as surely as, say, technology, or the social status of women, or European relations to the rest of the world. It has changed in its own musical way, but also in a manner that parallels changes in society. For a composer to adopt uncritically the musical form and language of an earlier age suggests a deliberate act of historical dressing-up. Of course, this raises the question of why it should matter when music is written. How can a musical language wear out? If it does, why do we persist in valuing old music and rejecting more recent music written in a similar style? The answer is that, with rare exceptions, new music written with an old language is a quite different proposition from the older music on which it draws. We do not have today the same tension between the means of expression and the expressive content. We can learn the clichés and the formulas, but we lack the invention that lifted the work above mere convention, not because we have less creative or original minds but because we live in a different world; the universe of artistic possibilities has irrevocably changed, as has the world that shapes our sensibilities. Someone who lives in a world shaped by electricity and computer technology, who has heard Wagner, Stravinsky, Duke Ellington, and Nirvana, does not respond to the inherent tensions of a sonata form in the same way as Haydn, or to the relation between major and minor as did Schubert.

Few musicians deliberately try to write music this way, even those who deliberately borrow aspects of older music. My interest is rather with music that purports to be of the modern world and to deal with modern sensibility and thought while nevertheless being profoundly indebted not only to an archaic musical language but often to a simplified form of it. In various ways, much of the musical culture that surrounds us derives its basic musical procedures from a much earlier age, a fact well illustrated by the music we encounter in film and TV. What is striking is not so much that in its essential vocabulary and syntax much of this music derives from the late nineteenth century, but that its expressive devices have become normative. We do not question their appropriateness or authenticity in representing narrative or carrying emotional content even in a film with a contemporary setting.

Normative music, defined above all by its melodic and tonal materials, has simply bypassed musical modernism as if it had never happened. Since our culture is saturated by the normative, to encounter music whose processes and materials are genuinely modern can be disorienting. This is one reason modern music continues to bewilder if not to shock: it lays bare a historical disjunction that we normally evade. That evasion is embodied in dominant culture by a music whose surface of technological complexity stands in an odd, contradictory relation to the simplicity of its basic musical materials. The underlying materials and formal patterns of much music made today are not just simple but archaically so.

Neither simplicity nor archaism are problematic in themselves. What *is* problematic is the masking of these qualities by a veneer of technological modernity. The disparity between outward form and inner content easily becomes a deception: the music seems to propose something that is utterly modern and expressive of the contemporary world. And yet, for all the impressive array of computer manipulation and electronically generated sounds, its musical proposition is essentially simplistic, often characterized by the repetition of its already undeveloped materials. Because the outward technological means are of primary importance, the fetishization of the sound-world, the performers, and the style position that they represent can easily obscure an underlying musical inanity. To return to my analogy of children's books, it is as if a prosaic proposition—"Janet likes John. John likes Janet"—becomes profound or exciting simply by being projected onto a vast screen by computer-controlled lasers. The extreme restriction of vocabulary and syntax prevents the text from delving into a greater sophistication of thought or feeling. In its place, one savors the intoxicating pleasure of being overwhelmed by the force of the technological means. The computer game is emblematic, employing a technological sophistication unimaginable even a decade ago in order to provide us with an experience that, for all its visceral excitement, is significantly less complex than a game of chess.

One could argue that the power and importance of these contemporary forms lie in their more bodily, libidinal energies and a communication that bypasses the literary models I have used. The technological aspects of these forms should, therefore, not be separated as a mere vehicle for a quasi linguistic content. My objection is not to the immediacy of the bodily or to the libidinal economy of pleasure in which we all have a stake, but rather to their dominance in cultural life and the way they squeeze out other kinds of experience, other sensibilities and ways of being. They do so partly by sheer saturation but also by their definition of the contemporary in which alternative practices such as art have no place. What should concern us about contemporary musical culture is the power it has to define the contemporary allied to the fact that it is based on a deception: a premodern musical language masquerading behind the latest technology.

Classical music thus finds itself in an ironic position. Despite its old appearance, classical music makes sophisticated and involved propositions about modern sensibility and thought that remain profoundly significant for our modern lives. It is nevertheless marginalized because it is based on relatively simple technological means. Dominant musical culture, on the other hand, becomes a key signifier of modernity because it employs the latest technological means while exhibiting simplistic, derivative musical means designed to avoid complex propositions. Doubly ironic, perhaps, is the fate of musical modernism: music that developed directly out of the classical tradition is dismissed as nonsensical, precisely because it has remained faithful to the historical tensions and intellectual demands of an earlier musical language. Conversely, today's normative music bypasses the intellectual achievements of our musical history. Why have we collectively refused the sophistication of thought and feeling embodied in an earlier language? And why, in its place, do we locate the height of modernity in a normative music confined to monosyllables and repetition?

More than a century after its beginnings, musical modernism is little liked and even less understood. Few cultural phenomena can have been so little assimilated a hundred years after their production. This alone suggests that the music requires critical reflection. It is symptomatic of our age, with its demand that everything be immediately accessible, that what requires thoughtful reflection should be so violently rejected. Intellectual and cultural goods should, such logic runs, be as accessible as anything else in the market. Art's rebellion against this immediacy and accessibility provokes a retaliation by the market that inverts its usual logic and here treats exclusivity as economically worthless. "Difficult" modernist music makes almost everyone angry because it offends so obviously against the pseudo-democracy of the market, making itself inaccessible in a way that the market alone cannot overcome. The price it pays for this rebellion is to be silenced, because, in a musical world governed by commercial criteria, what doesn't sell simply isn't heard.

Contemporary composers are easy targets for both conservative critics and left-wing activists. It is not hard to caricature the composer of modern music. The unremitting difficulty of their music is clear evidence, begins a long list of charges, of an arrogant, high-handed elitism and a self-obsession that imagines the world owes them a hearing. Their refusal to compromise suggests that they don't care about the audience, have no real desire to communicate, and probably hold the audience in contempt for not understanding their music. The music is too intellectual and devoid of feeling, and if it has anything at all to say, then that concerns only the self-obsessed world of the composer. It is overwhelmingly white, male, and middle-class. The caricature is not hard to recognize; it has been a feature of musical comment for well over a hundred years. But there is another account of what modern composers do, one that deserves to be taken seriously even though the arts, like every other sphere of life, has its fair share of posers, charlatans, snobs, and self-publicists. In this account it is not so much the willful awkwardness of composers that explains modern music's direction, but the peculiar condition of modern society in the twentieth century and its attitude toward art. Unpopularity is not so much the choice of contemporary composers as it is their fate. It remains so as long as they choose to continue the tradition of classical music—that is to say, an art form that deals discursively, on its own specifically musical terms, with the construction of a complex subjectivity and its relationship to the demands of the whole. This has a fundamentally ethical impetus: to pursue a truthful musical mediation of social reality wherever it leads rather than capitulating to something more immediate and entertaining.

The demand that composers should say what they have to say in a more accessible language, however well meant, betrays a signal lack of understanding about art. Because in art, and music most of all, *what* is said is inseparable from *how* it is said. To change one's musical language is to say different things; music does not literally speak about the world, but it speaks about the framework of thought and feeling in which we deal with the world, and what different musical styles represent is, on one level, simply the presentation and development of different frameworks. Beethoven's *Pastoral Symphony* doesn't tell us anything about nature; it tells us about a particular way of being human, in part defined by how we construct ourselves in relation to our experience of nature. So when Debussy or Webern or Birtwistle write in a different way, they are not simply dealing with nature in different musical styles; they are offering us different insights into our collective understanding of what it is to be human in a different historical context.

Perhaps modern music and pop music are both disfigured because they are both extreme positions. The historical refusal of popular musical materials in serious modern music points to an essentially negative definition of itself: it defines itself by what it is not. Even the technical language describes it in terms of what it lacks: it is atonal and unmelodic and often seeks to avoid a clear sense of beat, line, chord, phrase structure, form, and so on. It has most certainly exaggerated its intellectual and logical aspects. It views unmediated musical instinct with suspicion, and while it has a preoccupation with the irrational, it deals with it primarily as the resistant force against which it ties down its rational structures. It is self-consciously bound up with tradition and history because its deformations are explicable only in relation to that history. It resists immediacy and thus asks much of its listener. Not surprisingly, such music is marginal. Its claim to value lies in its elaboration of uncommon meanings, in the fact that it speaks what is not spoken elsewhere in our musical culture. It opens up new musical spaces and articulates a subject that is insistently bodily (consider the centrality of sonority in modern music) but that does not relinquish the intellectual and the abstract and thereby avoids regression. By definition, it is involved with limits, redefinitions, and reformulations rather than making statements in the enclosed space of familiar musical terms. It resolutely avoids the everyday, which is why it is hard to take and unpopular.

Why does a work like Schoenberg's *Erwartung*, composed in 1909, still sound prohibitively modern to many listeners? It uses no electronic or computer technologies and yet seems harder to grasp than most music produced in recent years. One obvious reason is the degree of fragmentation it exhibits: a close listening reveals a complex web of small motivic fragments. Taken one at a time, they might be more easily comprehended as signs of lyrical self-expression, but heard in such a dense contrapuntal web, and apparently dissociated from one another, the result is hard to grasp. Why does Schoenberg's music exhibit so much fragmentation and complexity? It's worrying that such questions are hardly ever asked. Professional musicians and scholars perform or discuss this music as if the answer were self-evident; the public continues to reject it as "mad" and have nothing to do with it.

Why is Schoenberg's music the way it is? Because in his music the free development of an expressive subjectivity comes into extreme tension with the demands of the objective system in which it takes place. To put this in more specifically musical terms, the lyrical, melodic aspect parts company with the harmonic system in which it was formally grounded. Western music is founded on the relation between melody and harmony;

since the Renaissance the changing form of this relationship has encoded music's mediation of the changing relation between the individual and society. Melody has always been the vehicle of the individual, expressive subject, but in classical music it comes into a unique balance with the collective demands of harmony and musical form, a balance that embodies the democratic ideal of a collective whole arising from the sum of its individual interactions. Romanticism, a movement far less distinct from modernism than listeners imagine, is marked by the dislocation of the two, the increasing tendency of the individual subject to find itself at odds with the demands of the collective and thus alone, solitary, and alienated. The responses of nineteenth-century composers to this situation are plural: some music engages with this alienation, while others answer it with the creation of fantasy worlds, withdrawal, or "heroic" attempts to refuse this broken equation.

This is the legacy Schoenberg's generation inherited: an intense sense of individual subjectivity at odds with the systematic whole. Insistence on the inviolable individuality of the material is bought at the cost of the uniformity of the system. What sounds like incoherence in later romanticism and early modernism is in fact only the saturation of subjective lines. With hindsight, it should not be hard to hear in the music what is self-evident in society: the ideals of the inviolable individual on which modern democratic society has been founded since the Renaissance come under severe threat by the multiplication of modern economies and technologies. Art has two options here: the system or the subject. Both are inadequate.

The key idea is *dissonance*. Musicians understand that this is a historical rather than absolute term, one central to common practice tonal music of the last few hundred years. What many of us think of as "expressive" music derives those qualities in part from its use of dissonance—from the *Crucifixus* in Bach's B Minor Mass to the chromatic inflections of a Rachmaninoff piano concerto. We expect music to deal with dissonance because we expect it to connect to our emotional and mental experience, which exhibits patterns similar to those constructed in the play of dissonance and resolution. Dissonance in music is an index of identity and nonidentity, of the experience of separation and resolution. That the idea of dissonance changes in musical history is a reflection of a changing social reality in which individuals experience themselves differently.

People justly reject the idea that because society is dissonant, music should be so too. Music, like all art, does more than reproduce or reflect society. At its best, it offers a utopian perspective: it becomes critical by revealing a different possibility. But in doing so it also risks becoming superficial and sentimental, and "falsely" beautiful, in an escapist way. At its best, art manages to square the circle of offering an image of something different while nevertheless wrestling with the full dissonance of reality. Art music of the last two centuries takes on the dissonance of the real world and transforms it. In that way it has a redemptive function. Music which simply ignores that dissonance is untrue: it becomes superficial, escapist, pleasurable nonsense, merely sensuous, in denial of an intellectual element, and thus essentially regressive and childish. We, too, are all of these things, and every one of us has to balance this complex equation for ourselves. My point is not to question our right to individual choice but to question the ingrained cultural habits and expectations that marginalize the distinctive value of one of those choices.

THE NEW IN MUSIC

I want to consider newness not in terms of musical language or style but as a category created within the music itself. All artworks, even when they deal with outward reality, construct their own world. Artists have a unique formal freedom within the picture frame or between the covers of a book that is definitive of art's nature. This is perhaps most obviously true for music, whose link to outward reality is far less obvious than in representational art or literary forms such as the novel. At the same time, as any artist will tell you, the freedom of the artist is a relative concept: one works with the demands of the material, in tension with the material, but never arbitrarily. An artwork may seem to create its own world, but to be significant, that world requires a certain level of coherence. In other words, the parts of the work need to belong together in some meaningful way, such that the work as a whole makes significant sense. And yet nothing is rejected more swiftly as art than the purely predictable and mechanical; instead, the works we tend to value most exceed this basic requirement by somehow balancing the need for coherence with the unexpected, unexplainable element, the aspect that seems to transcend the conditions of the work while nevertheless remaining within it. Mere coherence—the much-talked-about "unity" of an artwork—may not be very interesting at all. Artworks have to be more than tautologies.

There is no formula for this elusive balance of conflicting tendencies. Romantic aesthetics referred to it through the term "genius," without coming any closer to explaining how it takes place. We can perhaps point to examples, and certainly we can recognize the difference between the unexpected and the merely nonsensical. In a temporal art like music, we often have to suspend our judgment as the work unfolds: what appears to be a nonsensical departure may be explained later. Beethoven's music is full of moments where a sudden interruption or odd turn is clarified much later in the piece. One can imagine music that, on the surface, does something very similar but then fails to explain the extraneous event or detail, using it merely for its superficial shock value.

When critics have dismissed works as mad and incoherent that have later been hailed as masterpieces (as happened to Beethoven, of course), they have usually failed to follow the larger process by which new elements are subsequently woven into the larger form; they have not been convinced that the challenge to the conventions of the whole has been adequately integrated. It is a difficult game, and every artwork that is more than tautology must play it. To introduce a new character, a new theme, or a new key always creates a compositional problem; it shifts the balance of the whole and forces the author or composer to rebalance the work so that the new element makes sense. The balance of repetition and new elements is a compositional problem with which no composer, no matter what their style, can avoid wrestling.

Listeners may remain unaware of the composer's careful construction, such that the work proceeds as if it were quite natural. Classical music exemplifies this illusion, exerting a power that persuades us to accept musical processes as if they were utterly natural. But this illusion has always been offset by the constructive aspect that is the invention of the composer. This, ultimately, is the difference between art music and folk music, and it is directly linked to the difference between a notated tradition and an oral one. Classical music defines itself through an artistic balancing act. Though based on clearly audible stylistic conventions, it nevertheless exhibits a musical "wit" by which these conventions are presented, reworked, threatened, bypassed, and somehow restored. For all its apparently simple surface, this music projects a subtle and complex play of wit, albeit one that engages the emotions as much as the mind. One follows the propositions it makes and is engaged by its quasi logical discourse, but at the same time one is arrested by its leaps from one thing to another, its elliptical and tangential connections. It often denies expectations and disorganizes our sense of progression or succession, only to make sense of such leaps later on. This technical feature accounts for the sense of exceeding the listener's expectations. The music exceeds the limits and boundaries it has established. The play between the two is definitive of classical music: the arresting sidestep to a distant key is made possible by the conventions that shape our expectations of harmonic direction.

This characteristic might be demonstrated in virtually any classical piece, though we tend to value most those works that find a particular balance of this quasi logic and its own transcendence rather than those that fill a formulaic pattern with unproblematic material. Highly valued works either show apparently prosaic material in a far more fascinating light (such as Beethoven's *Diabelli Variations*) or begin with problematic material (such as Beethoven's *Pathétique* sonata). One could compare a work like Beethoven's first *Rasoumovksy Quartet* (op. 59, no. 1) with a work by Reicha or Spohr to show that the former accrues canonic status for precisely these reasons. But the idea of exceeding limits is not something we hear in the work through some unconscious comparison with lesser work; transcendence is an immanent feature of the work itself. Above all, it has to do with newness. This explains why we may return time and again to the same piece, even one that might have been written two hundred years ago. Certainly, things are "made anew" by performance, but we all know that some things do not bear much repetition. What makes classics repeatable is not, ultimately, their status; it has to do with the immanent narration of newness that each performance of the work reenacts. The new in music is thus not literally new, or else it would wear out and cease to be new. It is an objective category of the musical work.

There is a paradox here: a piece of music over a century old has the potential to provoke an experience of radical newness. Moreover, the work seems able to provoke this experience on repeated hearings. The encounter with newness, in Bach, Berlioz, or Boulez, seems diminished neither by the age of the work nor the number of times we revisit it: newness is, it seems, a property of the work, derived from the work's transcendence of its own boundaries. It has nothing to do with contemporary style. Beethoven's music, I would argue, reveals the new far more potently than much music written since. Nor does it matter how radical or cutting-edge the composer was in his own time. Bach, often seen as a conservative figure, engenders this quality in a way that some of his more fashionable contemporaries did not. This is because the fashionable currency of the style matters less than the quality of the underlying idea (to borrow Schoenberg's famous opposition). Art music has always been bound up with the idea of transcendence, whatever its outward style, or at least with underlining the tension between something bounded and the transgression of those boundaries.

Certain classical composers emphasize this idea of crossing musical boundaries; the encounter of something new is presented as an act of transcendence. This is not merely some metaphysical interpretation on my part, but an objective fact of the musical text. A musical work proposes itself not only as a set of musical materials but, implicitly, as a set of rules; a piece thus becomes literally transcendent by crossing the boundaries it has itself set up. This can happen in outwardly obvious ways, such as the sudden introduction of a completely new sonority. In his orchestral work *Déserts*, Varèse interpolates three episodes of tape music that break the boundaries of the acoustic instruments. In his second string quartet, Schoenberg introduces a soprano to underline the newness of the tonal regions to which the work moves. Janáček, in his second quartet, *Intimate Letters*, produces some startling moments of transgression through new sonoroties while confining himself to the usual four instruments. At other times, musical works effect a more inward transcendent move through a sudden shift in harmony or the arrival of a radically new form of its material. Beethoven's *Diabelli Variations* provide good examples of the latter, as does Liszt's B Minor Sonata, which transforms its themes into multiple versions while still preserving their essential identity. Beethoven's music is full of unexpected harmonic shifts that take the piece off in a tangential direction: in the first of his *Rasoumovsky Quartets*, for example, the first movement seems to start repeating its opening section, only to embark instead on a rhapsodic new section in a quite unexpected key. At other times, music presents new material that seems to cut across the piece's earlier logic to convey a shift in plane, a sense of arrival, a new beginning. The emergence of the "oriental" flute theme in the final movement of Mahler's *Song of the Earth* is one such example.

Such moments are by no means a feature of all music and are not a prerequisite of musical value. But this capacity might help explain the particular value of the classical repertoire as opposed to other kinds of music predicated on other functions. This quality of newness, the product of exceeding limits and transcending boundaries, has a utopian function. It not only expresses or symbolizes a transcendent moment; it enacts one as the music unfolds. And by the same token, listeners drawn into the musical process do more than contemplate a symbol of transcendence; they participate in its enactment.

CHAPTER 6. CULTURAL CHOICES

The division of culture by the spatial metaphors of high and low may be regrettable but has informed cultural criticism for too long simply to be ignored. For its proponents, the origins of this division lie in religious ideas of a spiritual ascent from the earthly to the heavenly. In this model, the low is confined to the physical and material conditions of our animal existence, whereas the high is concerned with the spiritual. The low is mortal and ephemeral, whereas the high is immortal and eternal. For its opponents, on the other hand, the metaphor maps directly onto the class divisions that embody hierarchies of social power. Low culture is thus that of the oppressed, and high culture that of the oppressors. Low culture voices a refusal of oppression, however impotent, while high culture celebrates power and confirms repression in the aesthetic domain. The first interpretation, in its secular form, is that of idealism, which had a definitive philosophical influence on aesthetics; the second is that of historical materialism, which exerted a similarly definitive influence on sociology and cultural studies. The first insists on a formal understanding of art, but in downplaying social and historical categories, it is apt to appear politically reactionary. The second emphasizes the primacy of social and historical conditions but is apt to make the artwork itself peripheral.

My summary is crude, but it touches on a profound division in thinking about culture. I want to suggest that these apparently antithetical readings of the same hierarchy have a common root and that the opposing positions they represent may yet be overcome. But whether we are able or willing to do this hinges on our larger conception of what it is to be human. It has to do with how we conceive of ourselves—whether our being is exhaustively mapped by an empirical science or whether our creative, reflective, and affective capacities exceed what can be accounted for in that way. I have argued that classical music projects an understanding of being human based on the idea of its capacity to exceed itself. Over and again, in countless individual works, its model of humanity is defined by a quality of hope, a reaching of the imagination beyond the conditions of the present. This is not merely a matter of subjective response; the category of hope is objectively realized within the musical process. In this way, music projects a utopian content.

There is no doubt that classical music has served as a tool of class distinction. But to suggest, as does sociologist Pierre Bourdieu, that its claim to difference is derived *entirely* from this function exemplifies the inadequacy of a theory that never confronts musical works themselves. Bourdieu's position is based on a vision of humanity that art rejects. Seeking to reverse the entire project of aesthetics since Kant, Bourdieu argues that taste is based on an aversion to the "facile," by which he means the immediate, the bodily, and the simple. His logic is persuasive—as, for example, in his demonstration of how class distinctions are reinforced by criteria for the selection and presentation of food that have nothing to do with its nutritional value. It is true that classical music seems to avoid the more direct and often bodily pleasures of popular music, but is this rejection based on "disgust," as Bourdieu suggests? I want to suggest another interpretation: classical music finds expression for our experience of exceeding the immediacy of the bodily. Without losing sight of the simple, the bodily, and the raw, it projects a sense of transcending those origins and an aspiration to realize a being not confined to the bodily. It remains true that "taste," as an aesthetic category, may be employed in a hollow manner as a tool of class distinction; artworks continue to be abused in this way. But the distinctions artworks make within themselves have nothing to do with material and historical class divisions; they are the distinctiveness of a refined, subtle intelligence that the work projects as the quality of humanity in general. In rejecting the works rather than their social abuse, we collectively cut off our nose to spite our face. Classical music projects a content that exceeds the materials from which it begins: it projects something that arises from the patterning of its sounding materials, a form (of a melody, a phrase, or a whole piece) that is itself an intangible, ungraspable idea. The music is a process of thought that takes off from the tangible but is not restricted by it nor reducible to it. In this it mirrors ourselves, which we also conceive of as exceeding the bodily conditions of our being. We insist on being more than physical objects; we insist on our identity as something intangible and irreducible to physicality, even while our being is rooted in it. This is the humanist position from which classical music begins: its essence is found not in the physical but in the content it projects beyond its physical elements by means of their formal patterning. In doing so it elevates us from the bodily, not out of disgust for it—classical music is not short of dance, song, and desire—but precisely to celebrate our twofold nature, the tension of spirit and body that defines us. The subtlety, complexity, and refinement of classical music are not arbitrary ways of distinguishing those who participate in it from those who do not. They are the qualities a humanist culture has valued as the condition of our humanity, the qualities by which we have defined the humanist ideal to which we aspire: reflective thought, tempered passion, care for the particular balanced by awareness of the whole, imagination, self-determination, persistence in the face of adversity, freedom.

If classical music causes a certain unease today, it is because it resists a narrow-minded political correctness that smoothes over the very real tension between egalitarianism and a fundamental human aspiration. Its historical origins are in Enlightenment ideals of universal rights, political democracy, and the inalienable self-determination of the individual. Classical music of the late eighteenth century was distinguished from the baroque through its populism, marked by its simple melodic materials, clear symmetrical phrase structures, and transparent musical textures. But it was distinguished from the popular music of its own day by the fact that it does not leave these materials as it finds them. It takes up the ordinary, the immediate—the facile, perhaps—and generates a highly elaborated, sophisticated development, a presentation of the idea that in the immediate, individual material lies the seeds of a larger self-realization. What could be a clearer and richer statement of those humanistic principles of the Enlightenment, the principles on which our modern society is founded and which we still invoke as touchstones of our individuality and identity?

To reject classical music as elitist or irrelevant is to sell humanity short; it is to deny our own tension between immediacy and potential for self-development that is its driving force. To side instead with immediacy, with the facticity of the given, without acknowledging the potential for change, transformation, growth, or elaboration, is to opt for an impoverished kind of being. It is to choose a musical culture that celebrates a resistance to transcendence and a refusal of our definitive inner freedom. A more useful definition of high and low would have nothing to do with the outward classifications of music; rather, it would involve the extent to which music enlivens our twofold nature, our definitive sense of exceeding the physicality of our being. Because just as music can awaken this sense and even trace a pattern of transcendence, it can also have quite the opposite effect. Music can deny those qualities that define a humanist culture, insisting instead on the absence of freedom and capacity for self-development, obliterating the differentiation of elements that are the hallmark of thought and substituting them with repetition. It can become a celebration of inanity.

In a word, music can be "stupid," a term noted by Simon Frith as central to everyday dismissals of music that seems to demean our capabilities. Our different judgments about what is musically stupid arises in part from the different expectations among social groups about what music should be and do. A sociology of music might outline how different aesthetic criteria, and thus different musics, hold sway for various social and cultural groupings. But reporting social facts and critical reflection are not the same thing, and we should be wary of a slide into relativism. Much of the music that surrounds us acts as a kind of aural tranquilizer. So-called elevator music is not confined to elevators: music that expunges any unfamiliar element, any hint of complexity or self-development saturates the private and communal spaces of modern life. This music is inane, stupid, and empty in the same way that repetitive and undeveloped writing is stupid, full of clichés and non sequiturs, attempting to pass off empty and worn-out phrases as the vehicles of genuine thought and emotion.

I have suggested that different musics do different things not just because they are used or valued in different ways but because they are made in different ways and exhibit different properties and characteristics. The world presents us with a wide range of things that may be considered food, a diversity that is largely the result of cultural differences. At the same time, different foods are made of different things and do different things for us. We acknowledge that if our diet lacks certain elements, our bodies may suffer physically and deteriorate. At the risk of exaggeration, I want to suggest that different musics have the capacity to exert different effects on us in an analogous way. We underestimate the reach of music. We invest it with great power to move us, shape our feeling, express our emotion, and define a collectivity, but at the same time we continually dismiss it as a personal matter, not worthy of thought or serious debate. We can insist that music is "all a matter of taste" only because we suppose music has no relation to social reality, that it does not refer directly to the real world nor have any real effect in it.

It may be this widespread undervaluing of music's power in the social realm, rather than our liberal tolerance of difference, that lies beneath society's acceptance, on equal terms, of all musical styles. But if music can be as inane and demeaning as other cultural forms, perhaps we should be skeptical about the much celebrated pluralism of contemporary culture. Cultural pluralism seems to be the fulfillment of a democratic ideal—a sign of mutual respect, tolerance, and happy coexistence. Today's musical cultures reflect a diversity that seems to mark a perfect union of individual self-determination and market choice. But pluralism also masks what used to be a more obvious tension between the idea of a dominant culture and its antagonistic subcultures; indeed, the idea of a dominant culture was perhaps essential in focusing the critical antiestablishment stance of subcultures. Today's pluralism makes that much harder, because its capacity to integrate and appropriate almost any new style makes the polarization required by critical subcultures more difficult. This has an important consequence, which is that we end up treating all music as different brands of the same thing, considering that music in general fulfills certain functions. Which music one chooses is then simply a matter of choice—no more, no less.

We justly celebrate cultural diversity as a sign of a free, multicultural society, but we reduce the vast potential of certain cultural practices if we see them merely as outward signs of so many style choices. We understand music little if we treat it as an empty sign. Music does things for us and to us; different musics do different things. To be sure, the same music may have different functions for different listeners, just as a similar function may be served for different listeners by quite different music. But different musics lend themselves more or less well to different functions. Schoenberg's serial music is not great background music, Palestrina is not great dance music, the Spice Girls do not reflect on human mortality or transcendent divinity. Neither is it just that different musics lend themselves to different functions we might consider valuable: we need to dance as well as to be still. Music, like other artworks, positions itself in relation to everyday life. It confirms it, contradicts it, negates it, reworks it, makes itself more or less distant. As an imaginary realm it makes itself different from the everyday, but as a matter of degree. It can reproduce dominant assumptions and ways of being or it can critique them. Even where music seems outwardly critical and speaks of refusal and difference, it may be no more than graffiti on the prison wall if it merely rearranges worn and familiar materials. Art's claim is different: it is based not so much on its refusal of reality but on its capacity to embody alternatives. For this reason, music has an ethical dimension, and our use of music and the musical choices we make involve us in ethical decisions.

ETHICAL CHOICES

It is not easy to balance the practicalities of daily life, by definition mundane, with an awareness of being situated in wider frames of time and space. Nor do we always want to. Being human seems to entail living in tension between an awareness of partaking in something larger than ourselves and a simultaneous resistance to its deep-seated tug. Our nature, rooted in immediacy, alternates with a capacity to exceed the narrow confines of our selves. Whether religious or not, we oscillate between the particularity of our lives and a larger, more universal whole; our myths and rituals speak of this paradox, of finding ourselves mortal and yet partaking in the divine. This is the contradiction, no less acute in a secular world, that art addresses. It does so, as we have seen, not through some magical power or simply because it moves us, but because it traces within itself the lineaments of that contradiction. The capacity to exceed our limits is a basic condition of both art and humanity. It is for this reason that art is profoundly humane. Art opposes the inhumanity that results when that tension is reduced to either total immediacy and particularity or total abstraction and objectivity. Art does so because it is constructed around the same inner tension between the demands of the particular and the claims of the universal. It thus catches the tension at the heart of our humanity and offers it back to us as an object for contemplation. Our enactment of the artwork offers us the possibility of momentarily transcending that definitive tension.

This, I have suggested, comes close to defining what makes art special. It is not a characteristic of all cultural products, and the heady mix of contemporary culture offers us quite different alternatives. The tension art constructs itself around can be both painful and pleasurable. We know that many of the cultural choices we make are deliberately easier than the demands art makes of us. We choose things that deny that tension or else provide a false, too easily achieved resolution. We can recognize the music that works like a warm bath or the film whose happy reconciliation doesn't ring true, but sometimes they seem like easier, less troublesome options than the harder work that art requires. Our lack of energy here, our feeling exhausted by the rest of life, makes us particularly susceptible to the easier fare that proliferates through a mutually confirming cycle of need and satisfaction.

It is, of course, our individual right to choose not to be open to the experience of artworks. But it is a free choice only if it is an informed one: there is no freedom in rejecting what has been kept closed to us. Having cultural choice about art implies that we have encountered the thing about which we exercise choice. This makes questionable the assumption that the pervasiveness of today's dominant commercial culture is the result of our active choices. Many people are excluded from the possibility of an encounter with something genuinely different from the dominant commercial culture, but not because art itself is exclusive. Rather, art was allowed to become exclusive in the past and is allowed to remain so today. Historically, this exclusion is a by-product of social class and power that has traditionally been differentiated through participation in symbolic mediums such as art. Today, this continues to be the case only inasmuch as we collectively allow it to do so.

Art does, then, confront us with some important collective choices. These necessarily impinge on political, educational, and legislative spheres and thus exceed what we think of as the personal and individual. It is only the mentality of the marketplace, applied to culture, that defines art and music as entirely a matter of individual choice. And this mentality produces a strangely reduced idea of individuality, one defined simply by a particular arrangement of cultural products constructed as personal style. The equating of cultural choice with personal style signals the end of an understanding of culture as something related to objective spirit. Culture is not something you choose: it confronts you with an objective force. To be sure, it is a composite product of individual consciousness and is amenable to our own work upon it, but it is far from being a matter of choice. Culture is no more a matter of choice than having two legs or being subject to gravity is; one can no more reject culture than reject electricity or weather. And yet one *can*, because while culture seems to confront us like a natural force, it is patently a human product. It *is* possible to reject aspects of culture, but not from a neutral position. To reject a set of ideas—such as those enshrined in modern democratic principles—is possible, but it is not a neutral gesture. It places one in opposition. Our cultural choices position us in relation to one another and also in relation to the larger ideas of which cultural products are vehicles. That we misunderstand this deeper connection today is illustrated by our tendency to use phrases like "my philosophy" or ask, "What's your philosophy on such-and-such?" Philosophy is not a matter of personal choice like a brand of soup or cereal; it is an objective intellectual field, riven with tension between its different positions. To adopt a position without awareness of its place in a field of conflicting tensions has nothing to do with philosophy.

Music, despite its apparently subjective nature, is rooted in the same social objectivity. That this statement seems odd today is perhaps a sign of the degree to which, in cultural matters, our educational system confirms rather than questions the relativism of everyday life. Education in science and mathematics does not pander to mere opinion and personal preference; it doesn't allow you to carry on thinking that the world is flat or that men are more intelligent than women, or any other prejudice you might have absorbed. It challenges these ideas with the objectivity of scientific method. Nor do the humanities pander to opinion. Students in the humanities and social sciences may not learn unequivocal facts about the world, but the works, events, and theories of these fields retain a level of objectivity. The works of Freud or Marx may be disputed, but they remain important facts of our cultural history: they cannot simply be ignored or dismissed as "not to my taste." Our world is a different place after aesthetic modernism, if only because of the skyscraper. It is meaningless to dismiss as a matter of taste ideas that shape the world.

Education is a collective choice enshrined in social legislation and provision. But it is unlikely to be effective where it is completely at odds with the society it serves. Granted, it must be in tension with society, because an educational system should express the aspirations of a society. But it should neither blatantly deny social reality nor simply reproduce it. A completely academic education with little connection to the student's world risks irrelevance, while a completely practical, "vocational" training risks reducing the student to a tool for future employment. Music is a good case in point. Those who teach music in schools and colleges have found it increasingly difficult to defend the relevance of the classical repertoire. In a multicultural society, classical music has inevitably become one repertoire among many, but in a way that reinforces the illusion of market choice. Students actively resist classical music because it is not "their" music—because it strikes them as belonging elsewhere. French may not be "their" language, yet it is not phased out: its otherness to students' culture is the reason it is on the syllabus. Our history is accepted as relevant because of its bearing on our present society; one does not reject studying the French Revolution because it is not "my" society. So why do we see this limited attitude toward culture, particularly toward music? Because music's place in cultural history is eclipsed by the overwhelming insistence on its function as personal pleasure—a problem that French, history, or geography do not face.

There is something suspect about a music education that focuses overwhelmingly on the music people consider their own. An education policy is dead in the water if it does not make room for an encounter with the new, with what initially exceeds the student's grasp. Geography lessons may begin with a focus on students' own locality, but they surely do not stop there, any more than history lessons deal only with students' present. What makes the music teacher's job so difficult is, paradoxically, students' attachment to music. Because schoolchildren, at a very young age, use music as a powerful vehicle of self-identity, their reaction to genuinely other music is not just indifference but often hostility. For those brought up on popular music, with little or no exposure to classical music, the latter is almost always identified with an older, more conservative generation, if not with a certain privilege. In a word, it's not cool.

Music educators occupy a difficult position. Their attempts to introduce students to something that, outside the classroom, they are unlikely to encounter let alone engage with, are resisted not only by students in the classroom but, increasingly, are opposed from outside the classroom, too. A wider academic self-doubt about the claims of classical music has an obvious effect on music education. The new style is eclectic and plural—by celebrating everything, one offends nobody. Thus, the education system reproduces the marketplace: it presents students with a multiplicity of choices but, all too often, without the deeper analysis of those products that would make choice a meaningful activity.

The embattled state of music education and a widespread social ignorance about music relate to one another like chicken and egg. Classical music has traditionally thrived as a social practice, not just as a product. Those who have engaged most profoundly in classical music have almost always practiced it themselves. Scratch the surface of most music lovers and you will often find an amateur musician, however lapsed their actual involvement. Amateurs, not professional musicians, keep classical music alive. And those amateurs, whether they sing, scrape, or blow, have developed their relationship with music in part through their active engagement. Overwhelmingly, this begins at school—with learning to play an instrument, playing in bands and orchestras, and singing in choirs. The signal failure of our educational system to fund this option properly is almost single-handedly responsible for the elitism of which classical music is itself accused. Why is participation in classical music elitist? Because only parents with sufficient financial capital and a certain educational background are likely to fund and encourage their children to participate in it. State education policy thus reinforces the social divisions it pretends to oppose.

Beyond the school gate there are signs of greater efforts to make classical music accessible. Almost every symphony orchestra and opera house now has an education department engaged in outreach programs. School-children work with composers and professional performers; new music ensembles play in prisons. Without detracting from what is often excellent work, I would suggest that such efforts remain drops in the ocean as long as society remains collectively disenfranchised from part of its richest musical heritage. This has to do with political and legislative choices such as education and the state subsidy of the arts. But this is not my theme. I am less concerned about the price of tickets to the symphony concert and the opera than the fact that people prefer to spend their money elsewhere. The state has a role to play in preserving a cultural choice that should be freely available to all. But ultimately it is a choice we make for ourselves.

The collective choices we make about music are the sum of our individual choices. School music teachers will always be swimming against the tide if the classroom is the only context in which children experience classical music. Educational crises are only particularly focused social ones. If we bemoan the low level of literacy among those who leave school at age sixteen or eighteen, we must also indict ourselves for creating a culture in which literacy counts for nothing. Who values literacy in a world where the TV replaced the book decades ago? Who values the demands of art in a world where every ubiquitous outlet of our dominant entertainment culture offers us something easier?

The idea of individuality is bound up with the idea of responsibility—to oneself as much as to others. To talk of individual choice without this attendant notion of responsibility is a dangerous deception—precisely the one made ubiquitous by the dominance of a marketplace mentality. Our fierce defense of our right to individual choice stems from a confusion of two things: our just passion for our individuality and our deception by the consumerist illusion that our choices have no effect on us or anyone else. In ignorance, we can act against our interests and those of others. Before medical research into the links between smoking and cancer, generations of smokers damaged themselves and others in innocence. But with greater knowledge comes ethical responsibility.

To talk of ethics in the same breath as art or entertainment sounds suspiciously puritanical. But it is salutary to remember that a generation ago ethical questions about our food choices might have seemed equally inappropriate, while today it is quite normal to consider not only how our food is produced but where it comes from, who makes it and under what conditions, and what it does to us. We are concerned not only with whether food is "good for us" in a physical sense, but also with ethical questions about the power of multinational corporations in the Third World, the environmental effects of industrialized agribusiness, and the long-term dangers of biotechnologies like the genetic modification of crops. We may think about these issues to varying degrees, but most of us accept that it is reasonable to think about our consumption of food in these ways. Caught in the immediacy of our lives, we face no obvious ethical question in the supermarket: we hurt nobody by purchasing the product on the shelf before us. But the greater knowledge we now possess, however patchy, impinges on such opaque immediacy, and the wider ecological and social context of the product before us may begin to inflect the choices we make as consumers. What was merely a pound of coffee before now becomes a link in a chain that goes back to the conditions of Nicaraguan workers and the exploitative relationship between Western-based multinational companies and the producer country. To refuse to make those choices is to refuse something of the claims of democracy. It is to prefer to mingle with the crowd because it's easier than the responsibility of independent reflective thought, judgment, and action.

As a society, we accept a ban on smoking in public places once we understand the risks of passive smoking. Had the ban been introduced without the publicity about passive smoking, this would have seemed like a dictatorial invasion of private choice. Is it implausible that one day we might look at cultural products, such as music, with the same increased awareness? It seems unlikely, because here the criteria lack the factual authority of medical research. And yet many of us feel uncomfortable watching scenes of apparently gratuitous violence and recoil at materials that are openly racist or sexist. This is not just about moral correctness or political persuasion: it goes back to our refusal to be demeaned, our refusal to be addressed in ways that make us less than we are. But if visual and literary representations can be thought of this way, music seems to resist it entirely. And as long as we think of music solely in terms of individual pleasure, the idea that our participation in music might involve ethical choices is hard to accept. But perhaps only our lack of understanding makes it seem far-fetched that music involves us in dynamics that are equally (if invisibly) positioned. It is not that we should not have musical choices but that we should have the awareness to make informed choices. Cigarettes carry government health warnings, and we all make informed choices about the dangers and benefits of what we eat and drink. Increasingly, we demand that appropriate information be made available so that we can make these choices. Why are we so concerned about food additives, the presence of genetically modified crops, or the lives of battery hens and yet so utterly unconcerned about the content of the cultural products with which we feed our minds?

Legislative choices about education and state subsidy for the arts are properly collective ones. But their ability to bear fruit hinges on our individual choices. What we do and what we value individually become collective actions and values. Why do we so often fail to choose what we claim to value? Perhaps because we do not carve out the space to stop and think. It's hard to step out of the spin cycle of one's life and question its habitual patterns. All this seems like it might be possible if only we could find some space (temporal and spatial) for these things—but that space seems to be forever eluding us. The paradox is that, while art certainly requires us to give it some space to work, it is one of the most potent ways to create space in our lives. We do have to make a practical choice—to carve out thirty minutes, or sit quietly in another room and retire behind the headphones—in order for art to have the space to breathe. But the result is often an experience that makes a metaphorical space whose weight and intensity far exceeds the time we give to it.

Perhaps the most important cultural choice we face today is that between distraction and contemplation. The first has to do with entertainment functioning as avoidance, and the second has to do with engagement and a deeper involvement. It's no coincidence that the term
"contemplation" is shared by art and religion: the contemplative attitude
points to a way of being that is essentially open to the encounter with an
Other. I am not suggesting that engagement with art requires us to live
like monks or nuns; but I am suggesting that our lives are poorer for the
lack of this level of engagement. Nor do I blame the ills of modern society on television; our dependence on this narcotic distraction is undoubtedly a symptom rather than a cause. What is frightening about the bulk of
TV and radio is not that we are drawn into its twenty-four-hour cycle of
inanities—no doubt we all need some inanity—but that this empty patter
becomes normative. The lack of space for other ways of being and the exclusion of other kinds of feeling or understanding are what make the
dominant media and their dominant content so questionable. It is not the
thing itself that threatens our capacity to be fully alive, fully developed
human beings; it is the exclusive function the dominant media come to
have in our lives. They come to define a whole way of thinking, a horizon
of expectation, a way of behavior, a way of engaging with the world that
leaves no room for others. Sociologists used to talk of a dominant culture,
by which they meant a conservative and canonic notion of traditional culture against which various movements in popular culture might be judged
as subcultures or even countercultures. Today that analysis no longer
holds true. Dominant culture now is defined by mainstream, homoge-
nized popular culture that nobody really identifies with but virtually
everybody participates in.

Music plays a central role in this entertainment culture, and for many
people that includes classical music. But to function *as art*, classical music
requires a different set of conditions. It requires a contemplative attitude
that the distraction culture explicitly forbids. Art does not easily thrive in
the division of life into work and those ends of days and weeks into which
we cram our not-work—time that, for many people, is no less stressful than
work. Adults overburdened with responsibility at work and home look to
their leisure time as a space in which to stop being responsible—to play, to
become childlike. We don't want our leisure activities to be intellectually
demanding precisely because leisure is defined as a release from such responsibilities. Our lack of engagement with serious art is by no means unconnected to our work lives, which impose a certain expectation about our
leisure time. We end up caught between two extreme positions: the high-
pressure round of adult responsibilities and the times in which we persuade

ourselves that we can take a break from being an adult. The extremity of the division is insidious; to escape it requires more self-determination than most of us usually have the energy for, let alone the inclination.

But the presence of art poses central questions and forces us to acknowledge that certain existential choices are our responsibility. Art is an irritant; its silent insistence on something other challenges our passive acquiescence to a life of filling the vacant spaces left to us between work hours. Art challenges the identity we create through work and responsibilities to other people; it forces us to ask who we are when we stop doing these things so busily. Art encodes something of the vastness of the human mind and spirit, a vastness that mirrors that of the external world, of the night sky or the depths of the oceans. We can choose to engage with it, to allow our minds and spirits to resonate through it, or we can choose to fill the empty spaces of our lives with game shows and TV shopping channels.

The plural products of contemporary culture are not neutral, nor are the individual and collective choices we make. My concern is not just that the claim of classical music to embody an essentially humanist aspiration is drowned out by much that is nonsensical, demeaning, and empty; it is that much of what passes for the dominant culture constitutes a denial of those aspirations of humanity. My charge is thus more serious. It is that, individually and collectively, we often allow a significant disjunction between our moral, political, and spiritual values and our cultural choices. One objectively contradicts the other, a fact of which we are blissfully but dangerously unaware, because we no longer think about art and music. That we can espouse liberal, humanist ideals such as individuality, democratic freedom, and self-realization and yet participate, often exclusively, in music whose content objectively contradicts these ideas is a paradox both individual and social. The irony is that our uncritical faith in pluralism as a product of the marketplace, a faith that seems to embody the idea of individuality through choice, objectively undermines our humanist ideals.

Cultural choices are ultimately ethical choices. That we generally do not understand this is both a sign and a result of a contemporary neutralization of culture. It seems politically correct to abstain from judgments about music, yet the social and ethical responsibilities that inform our notion of individuality are based on our ability to make objectively binding judgments. Today, ironic distance and a deliberate avoidance of committing oneself to a position of judgment seem liberal and cool. This masquerades as democracy and community, but in reality, in its laissez-faire relativism, it is the absence of community or democracy: it is a pseudo-community that arises from the anxiety of not knowing whether anyone else thinks the emperor is naked and from believing oneself to be more genuinely part of the community because one maintains the same critical silence as everyone else.

ENACTMENT

To say that art implies the priority of the work over our perception is not to say that we have no role in contemplating artworks. It is that our experience of art is richer when we are sufficiently quiet to let it speak. What may often be seen as the stuffiness of art and a pretentious awe that surrounds it is only the outer edge of an approach that allows art the space and silence to be heard. In the case of music, that requirement is structured by the time in which music takes place. As listeners, we connect with its unfolding process only to the degree that we allow ourselves to be carried within its current. In doing so, we parallel the activity of the performer, who has no choice but to move with the music and to follow with care its every change of pace, direction, tone, and manner. Listening is thus also a taking part, a performative action, a kind of doing.

Earlier, I considered how, in spite of its temporal nature, music can function like an object. Music, which is not an object at all, is transformed into one through the technology of recording. And while in theory this should leave its performative potential unchanged, in fact it displaces this claim of music from the central position it once held. Technology allows uses of classical music that are at odds with the temporal propositions of the music itself. It makes such uses not only possible but increasingly dominant: the fact that one can pause the symphony to answer the phone means that one probably will. This object-use of music works against its capacity to function as art, because what matters about art is not so much the object but the activity it engenders. So much of the energy surrounding art today seems to focus on the object at the expense of the activity. We have become obsessed with artifacts at the expense of art. The huge financial value placed on original artworks (and certain performers) is only a holdover from a time when artworks were invested with very real power to transform those who came into contact with them. If that transformation ceases to take place, the financial value is merely fetishistic and may yet evaporate, leaving artworks worth no more (financially) than the canvas they are painted on. Where art ceases to provoke a certain kind of activity in its recipient, it fails to function as art: the encounter that constitutes the idea of art fails to take place.

Art is a particular form of our poetic capacity—of the quintessentially human act of remaking the world. But this is an activity, not a thing. Poetry, understood properly, is not a text one can place in the library, not an artifact, but an event: something that happens when a connection is made that places the material in the context of the nonmaterial. The danger of our academic-museum culture is that it joins forces with a materialist culture in focusing on objects rather than how we use them, what we do with them, or what we allow them to do with us. To be sure, the object remains important, but its possession is no guarantee that one "has" poetry. A defining paradox of art is that it is the result of *poesis*, the making of forms, while being an object whose specific value is the transcendence of its own object nature. And that transcendence occurs as a result of our engagement with the object, an active contemplation that is also a kind of *poesis* in real time. To develop this skill, we need not so much education "about art" as education "in art," not academic learning but the acquisition of ways of approaching art—ways of being open, receptive, patient, humble, and nonliteral. These are signs of a different approach to the artwork, a different expectation of what art is and does.

Approaching music differently means living differently. Our contemporary object-use of music is a product of our lifestyle. Ironically, we think our standard of living so high and advanced compared to that of others around the world and that of our ancestors, yet we have no time to properly contemplate anything at all. A contemplative mode of being is essentially denied to our generation. We have unprecedented potential freedom, but we are often overwhelmed by the sheer number of possibilities, mesmerized like deer in the headlights. It is hard, even for those of us who pay lip service to the idea, to make the deliberate focus that such an approach requires.

It would be foolish to speculate how this fundamentally human activity might once again find a place in our lives. Our secular, material society seems to exclude it entirely. And yet the desire for contemplative space is evident all around us, for all that it is often fobbed off with the merely stylish. The stripped-down, calm minimalism of the design magazine article is rarely the product of a genuinely spiritual life and, bought off the rack, is unlikely to deliver one. To be sure, marketers feed this hunger just as they create it: the absence of contemplative space in our lives becomes yet another lack that can be filled by a marketable product. In this way, classical music seems to revive as one of several lifestyle products whose possession promises us the depth of being that the rest of our lives seems to exclude: its new niche is in compilations of "relaxing classics" found in the garden center next to books on Feng Shui and herbal massage.

What marketers sell as a "new spirituality" preys on a genuine hunger. But it is false because it passes off *things* as substitutes for a state of mind and a way of life. We run the risk of equating spirituality with relaxation, a context in which the spiritual claims of art are also distorted. Spirituality, whether in a religious context or the secularized medium of art, is not without its trials and oppositions, not without its sufferings. Above all, it is a lived process, a path, rather than a sporadic collection of momentary revelatory experiences had along the way. The marketing of spirituality may be the lowest point in the spiritual health of our age, just as the marketing of classical music as relaxation may signal the end of classical music's serious function as art. As relaxation, it becomes one with the aromatherapy candles and the bath oil: it is a way to achieve temporary release, a switching-off.

To say that without the process of enactment, no art takes place—that art is not an object but an activity, an engagement between the affective consciousness and self-contained, significantly structured objects—is not to undermine the importance of the art object but to insist that the object alone is not enough. It is to say that without us, no art takes place. This is indispensable if we are to overcome the fetishism attached to art objects. There is no inherent value in simply surrounding oneself with great music and art; what matters is the degree of exposure one is prepared to give, accompanied by the going out of the receptive mind, the active encounter with the object. The fetishism of art objects has not helped art's cause at all. Attributing value to the object rather than the encounter underlies the arrogant dismissal of so many works. "If I don't get it, it's no good" is a mind-set that will never understand art because it fails to understand that art requires a humility and patience in the face of the object—and not mere passivity either, but an active opening of our responses.

The contemplative space that art demands is at odds with a highly functional, practical, profit-driven society. That is why art has always been seen as superfluous by the practical-minded and puritanical. Art-as-object can find house space as part of the sign system of contemporary "style," but art-as-activity is at odds with today's dominant ethos. Traditionally, the superfluity of art and the unproductive nature of time spent "doing" it predispose it to serve as a sign of aristocratic or bourgeois luxury and freedom from necessity. But doesn't sport fulfill a similar function? Isn't the freedom to play one of the most profound expressions of our humanity? And isn't the freedom from outward necessity that art symbolizes an expression of one of our most deep-seated aspirations? Music also (like sport) offers an activity that is not generated by means-end logic, that redeems the individual life as rich in itself, not for some other function. The play music offers is perhaps one of the highest activities of humankind: without outward purpose but profoundly meaningful.

In music we enact what is palpably unreal, yet it strikes us with a force that reality often does not. That is why we invest music with the power to bring out aspects of our being that our outward lives often prohibit and exclude. This is the contract we make with art: that by entering its unreal, fairytale world of illusion, we access aspects of our being of which the one-dimensional understanding of material common sense has no conception. As long as the enactment lasts, we partially live the illusion art plays out for us. To be sure, art may be judged escapist, narcissistic, even infantile in its play and ideological in its false promise of happiness. But it is also utopian, and it leaves us altered, tinged with a memory that things might be different or that things once were different.

Classical music rarely offers a literal representation of a utopian, harmonious, and reconciled society—although the massed collective voices of a symphony orchestra and chorus clearly speak in the plural. The voice one hears in a Bach *Passion* or in Verdi's *Requiem* is a collective "we" rather than the voice of the composer. But classical music often presents a *metaphor* of reconciliation, one that expresses the complex competing voices of the self and society. Consider a string quartet: its competing voices unfold in relation to one another—now one, now another gaining the upper hand. In their polyphonic exploration of the different aspects of the same material, they mirror our plural voices and those of the social whole. Not only does the performance thereby present a metaphor, an abstract model for contemplation; the musical work also invites, or even demands, participation through enactment. Live performance makes visible the outer surface of a largely inward activity. To watch a string quartet perform is to witness a complexity and refinement of interaction that is matched by very few human activities. The exchange between musicians is characterized by a sensitivity, sophistication, and elaboration that articulates the limits of human potential. The interaction heard in the music, and enacted physically in the gestures of the musicians is both intellectual and emotional and something else at the same time. It has to do with a quality of mutual care, respect, and understanding, with being part of a collective and yet independent. Each part has a particularity, an identity established and simultaneously transcended in its relation to other parts. From this interaction of individual freedom and togetherness arises something that exceeds the limits of the everyday. It is a metaphor for the best and most cherished human activities and characteristics.

The listener, too, enters into this process of enactment, but not one focused on a particular voice or part—something more akin to the activity of the conductor, who enacts the piece in all its polyphonic complexity without actually generating a sound. The listener enacts the sum of all that we have credited this music with. Because music abstracts and internalizes the idea of limits and boundaries, it makes possible the enactment of their transgression. Because music internalizes space and time, it allows us to enact their transcendence, which is why music has a uniquely intense ability to summon up what is distant or long past.

Music-as-art shapes our perception of the world, not by pretending to speak of the real world but by its construction of imaginary others. It sheds light on our present reality precisely by being conspicuously different from it. This music resists the everyday because its function is to be Other. If we resist this music, it is because we lack the capacity to live with the tension between what is and what might be, between the real and the imaginary. Art transforms reality in order to keep alive the possibility that it might be otherwise, and thus art is an agent of social critique and of individual transcendence. The way art treats its materials implies that its content lies elsewhere, *through* its materials but at the same time *beyond* them. This is what is meant by form in art—something constructed in the patterning, the sum of the relationships constructed by the work's unfolding materials. Its content, while rooted in the material, sonorous aspects of the music, can be grasped only by an activity of the mind. In this way, classical music affirms a fundamentally humanist vision.

Of course, while both the performer and listener enact the piece, we respond to the process in different ways. A piece of music is more like a landscape in which we find different paths than a map with compulsory routes, junctions, and viewpoints. But a landscape is not an entirely subjective construct: it confronts us with objective, material facts (like mountains and rivers) that we respond to in making our path through it. And more often than not, the landscapes music presents are highly suggestive of the ways we might perceive them and travel through them. Because the form one enacts (in per-forming or listening) is not one's own form but that shaped by the music. Even though the performer generates the sound, the piece "has a life of its own" to which both performer and listener are bound. Both enact something that has an ontological priority over one's responses and efforts. Music-as-art thus realizes its most distinctive value, one that materializes only in response to the setting aside of the subjective demands and priorities of the listener. Only when one has stopped making demands of the musical object, silenced one's own discursive chatter, can the music begin to exert *its* demands on the listener—to go here now, to recall this, to feel this way, to deal with both of these ideas at once, to wrestle with this protracted uncertainty.

To lose oneself in music is not uncommon. Music's capacity to affect us this way leads most of us to invest it with power. But the philosophically opaque idea of losing oneself masks a variety of responses. One can lose oneself in drunkenness or sleep, a shutting down of one's capacity for reflexive thought and feeling. But losing oneself in music or art, however briefly, is characterized by a heightening of these capacities, an intensity of feeling and mental activity that is the product of entering into the object's demands. This is different from the awe with which one might gaze on a view in nature; the artwork involves one in an activity that is not static but responds in time to the work's discursive journey. One is taken aboard and embarks on an intellectual journey that exceeds one's own imagining.

Not only does music offer the possibility of transcending daily life; it offers, in as many forms as there are musics, a reshaping of those categories. It doesn't obliterate them in some narcotic emptiness but reworks them and thus offers us new models of experience. And this has a real power, because as we participate in this process of enactment, we experience new ways for ourselves. When we leave the musical work and return to daily life, we have tasted a different way of being, a different perception of the world. Potentially, this leaves us marked by the experience. It subsequently produces an altered perception of the world.

This aspect of aesthetic experience is much contested. For some, the realms of art and reality have no connection whatsoever. Aesthetic experience is fantasy and has no bearing on reality. A certain kind of behavior refuses its challenge to the everyday or treats it like an escapist drug to indulge in from time to time without imagining that it affects real life. This has often inclined its addicts to melancholy in the face of a world that is not as art portrays it. At the other extreme are those who would make real life like art. But there are other, less extreme or dogmatic reactions. Many people know that vague sense, on leaving a concert, that we have not only seen a different world but experienced the possibility for ourselves. And though this lingers as an aftertaste, a memory, it can disturb us in subtle but powerful ways like the memory of a dream. We don't discover the content of that dream in daily reality, but the dream may nevertheless make us see reality in a different light. This will not necessarily change our actions, but it can certainly change our perception of the world and thus our attitudes and so even, in time, our actions as well.

But if music has such power and is at the same time a varied thing, then one must reflect on what *different* musics do. If music reworks the categories of everyday life, it can surely do that to a greater or lesser extent. Some musics may come close to reproducing the pattern of limits in everyday life, while others may depart radically from it. And some may reconfigure our perceptions in ways that seem attractive (exciting, reassuring, challenging), while others seem rather negative (threatening, depressing, undermining). This brings us back to the question of what different musics do and how different pieces or different styles reconfigure the familiar.

The value of music-as-art lies in a difficult balancing act between the particularity of its materials and the abstract idea that it projects through their patterning and reworking. Its goal is to treat the materials in such a way that they do not lose their particularity, while at the same time, through their configuration, point beyond their particularity. As music, this process is played out in time, through an unfolding that mirrors the way we define our subjectivity. This is more than metaphysical nonsense: it is a squaring of the circle that we claim as fundamentally human. We understand ourselves as particular, physical beings, but we also value the ways we exceed the physical, the ways our capacity for thought, feeling, and imagination seem to transcend our bodily existence. Music-as-art performs a similar alchemy: in projecting a content beyond its acoustic materials, it does not deny its physical aspect but redeems it as the vehicle of something that exceeds the physical. In doing so, it offers us not only a symbol of our transcendent nature but also a means for its repeated enactment. Its value is both personal and social: it mirrors within itself the constituent processes of a complex subjectivity and also projects the ideals on which modern democracy is founded. But its ability to function in these ways hinges on the degree to which we remain, individually and collectively, alive to its potential. Our capacity to do so is ultimately an ethical question, one that impinges on both individual and collective choices. For music, as all art, does not work without us. It requires us to come out to meet it. Nothing happens without the inward motion we make toward it: a gesture of opening and anticipation, a willingness to embrace the encounter that music promises.

BIBLIOGRAPHY

Adorno, Theodor W. *Aesthetic Theory*. London: Routledge and Kegan Paul, 1984.
———. *Introduction to the Sociology of Music*. New York: Continuum, 1989.
Adorno, Theodor W., and Max Horkheimer. *Dialectic of Enlightenment*. London: Verso, 1979.
Baumol, William J., and William G. Bowen. *Performing Arts: The Economic Dilemma*. New York: Twentieth Century Fund, 1966.
Bergeron, K., and Philip V. Bohlman, eds. *Disciplining Music: Musicology and Its Canons*. Chicago: University of Chicago Press, 1992.
Bloom, Allan. *The Closing of the American Mind*. New York: Simon and Schuster, 1987.
Bourdieu, Pierre. *Distinction: A Social Critique of the Judgement of Taste*. London: Routledge, 1984.
Braden, Sue. *Artists and People*. London: Routledge and Kegan Paul, 1978.
Cook, Nicholas. *Music, Imagination and Culture*. Oxford: Clarendon Press, 1990.
———. *Music: A Very Short Introduction*. Oxford: Oxford University Press, 1998.
Einreinhofer, Nancy. *The American Art Museum: Elitism and Democracy*. London: Leicester University Press, 1997.
Frith, Simon. *Performing Rites*. Oxford: Oxford University Press, 1998.
Green, Lucy. *Music on Deaf Ears: Musical Meaning, Ideology, Education*. Manchester: Manchester University Press, 1988.
Hanslick, Eduard. *The Beautiful in Music*. Indianapolis: Bobbs-Merrill, 1957.
Hegel, Georg W. F. *Introductory Lectures on Aesthetics*. London: Penguin, 1993.
Hutchinson, Robert. *The Politics of the Arts Council*. London: Sinclair Browne, 1982.
Kant, Immanuel. *The Critique of Judgement*. Oxford: Clarendon Press, 1986.
National Endowment for the Arts. Mission statement at http://arts.endow.gov/learn/ [Web site].
Parakilas, James. "Classical Music as Popular Music." *Journal of Musicology* 3 (1984): 1–18.
Scruton, Roger. *The Aesthetic Understanding*. Manchester: Manchester University Press, 1983.
———. *The Aesthetics of Music*. Oxford: Oxford University Press, 1998.
Shaw, Roy. *The Arts and the People*. London: Jonathan Cape, 1987.
Small, Christopher. *Music, Society, Education*. London: Calder, 1980.
Steiner, George. *Real Presences*. London: Faber, 1989.

Swanwick, Keith. *Music Education and the National Curriculum*. London: Tufnell Press, 1992.

Tawa, Nicholas E. *Art Music in the American Society*. New Jersey: Scarecrow Press, 1987.

Thornton, Sarah. *Club Cultures: Music, Media and Subcultural Capital*. London: Polity Press, 1995.

INDEX

abstract thought, 48, 60, 74, 116
  in music, 20, 32, 40, 49, 55–56, 63, 69, 105
  See also music-as-thought
academics, 19, 20, 22, 31, 89, 92, 119
acoustic instruments, 6, 92, 110
Adorno, T. W., 25
adult culture, 45, 72–73
aesthetics, 21, 39, 107, 111–12
  of music, 6, 12, 15, 53
  See also philosophy
alienation, 68, 84, 93, 106
amateurs, 20, 38, 52–53, 119. *See also* performers
analysis, 51, 61, 73, 78, 82
aria, 27, 69, 75
art, the claims of, 5, 6–7, 8–9, 23, 31, 35, 51–52, 70, 93–95, 115–16, 122–23, 128
  and immediacy, 74, 88, 90
  social function of, 21, 47–50, 83–84, 120
art galleries, 23, 30, 47, 58, 91
artifacts, 47, 52, 56–57, 86, 91, 124
artificiality, 13, 89–90
Arts Council of Great Britain, 17, 19, 20, 85
arts policy, 17–26
artworks, 9, 48–49, 51–52, 56, 77, 80, 94–97, 107, 112, 124
aspiration, 5–6, 25, 49–50, 69–70, 88–90, 111–13, 123. *See also* human potential

Auden, W. H., 74
audience, 3, 22, 36, 40, 49, 68, 75–76, 81–82, 87–88, 98, 104
aura, 47, 86, 91
authenticity, 40–41, 48, 68, 82, 89–90, 93, 100, 102
authority, 12, 19, 24, 52, 74, 78
autonomy, of art, 20, 31, 33, 39, 52, 54, 63, 82, 92–93
  of individuals, 65
avant-garde, 33, 35, 50. *See also* modernism

Bach, C. P. E., 98
Bach, J. S., 34, 38, 53, 74, 93, 99, 109
  choral music, 67, 68, 106, 127
  Goldberg Variations, 69–70, 98
background music, 6, 33–35, 37, 51–54, 80, 98, 114. *See also* mood music
ballads, 35, 101
baroque music, 27, 35, 67, 70, 100, 113
Bartók, Béla, 74
BBC, 22, 75, 85
Beatles, 74
Beethoven, Ludwig van, 6, 38, 45, 46, 65, 67, 82, 93, 98, 107–8, 109, 110
  piano sonatas, 35, 53, 109
  symphonies, 75, 77–78, 104
Benjamin, Walter, 86
Berg, Alban, 75, 100
Berlioz, Hector, 99, 109
Birtwistle, Harrison, 45, 104
Bloom, Allan, 25